Praise for I Was Born in An Old Age Home

I am honored as well that I was able to read it. ... It is all in all an amazing (!!!!) testimony.

> Marc E. Brüggemann, M.A., Ph.D. candidate/ELES Research Fellow, Joint Ph.D. [The Hebrew University Jerusalem/Frei Universität Berlin], Topic: Jewish History in the 20th century

A powerful memoir – the story of a life well lived after a harrowing and lucky childhood escape from Germany and the Nazis. Sanne DeWitt writes a fascinating, sometimes tragic, but often humorous, tale of her long, improbable life. Highly recommended.

> Bill Mowat, Anti-Defamation League National Executive Committee Member

A life well spent. Sanne DeWitt delivers a personal story of perseverance and strength—from escape from Nazi tyranny to her husband's courageous fight against above ground nuclear testing and the challenges her family experienced with a drug addicted daughter. Well worth the read.

> Riva Gambert (Pitluck)

This is a fascinating autobiography, written with unusual openness about the author's and her dear ones' foibles, but also showing her and their strengths. The trials she goes through, the quirks of fate, make stimulating reading.

May she live to the proverbial hundred and twenty, enjoying her children's, grandchildren's and later great grandchildren's accomplishments.

I Was Born in an Old Age Home is about and by an extremely talented, accomplished woman.

Judith Ronat M. D

All memoirs reflect their authors' lives, but this book truly stands out. Sanne de Witt has been a witness to many key events in modern history. As a child, she was fortunate to escape the Holocaust. As a consequence, throughout her life she felt responsibility for other children who were not so lucky, and she did her best to prevent the tragic mistakes of the past from repeating. It is amazing to see in this must-read book how much a single person with noble and deeply felt intentions can accomplish.

Vladimir Kresin, Prof., Dr., Lawrence Berkeley Laboratory, University of California at Berkeley, CA

I WAS BORN IN AN OLD AGE HOME

A Memoir

SUSANNE KALTER DEWITT

Barany Publishing

Copyright © 2018 by Susanne Kalter DeWitt

Published by Barany Publishing, 771 Kingston Ave., Suite 108, Piedmont
CA 94611

Cover by Ezra Barany

Book Production by Beth Barany

Cover image: Oma (Grandma) Betty Katzenstein (about 75 years old) and Sanne
(Peterle, 2 years old) in 1936, photography attributed Uncle Ernst Katzenstein.

ISBN: 978-1-944841-17-1 (1st Print Edition)

ISBN: 978-1-944841-18-8 (1st E-Book Edition)

❀ Created with Vellum

Contents

"It's no challenge to die like a Jew, the real challenge is to live like a Jew."

The Chofetz Chaim

I dedicate this memoir to our children, Ralph, Joel and Laila and to our grandchildren, Raizel, Langley and Tenaya DeWitt. With much love and admiration for them, Grandma Sanne

Introduction

When I mention to friends that I am writing a memoir I often get the question: "What it is special about your life and why would anyone be interested in your story?" I feel that it is takes "chutzpa" to write a book about my life, and my experiences are part of history and should not be forgotten. That is the justification. I survived the early days of Nazi Germany, and my escape and subsequent adventures in various countries and situations are unique and interesting. Everyone's life story is unique but my experience of surviving the horror of the Nazi regime may be of historical significance.

The Nazis murdered over one million Jewish children, a horrendous tragedy. I am overwhelmed and grateful that I was able to escape. My parents courageously sent me out of Germany, perhaps never to see me again. We were lucky that our separation was temporary and that we survived as a family. In fact, we were very lucky and by the fifties, we had established a successful new life.

I am indebted to my parents, Dr. Samuel (Sami) Kalter and Klara Katzenstein Kalter, and all of the many wonderful people who helped me to survive.

~Susanne (Sanne) Thekla Regina Kalter DeWitt

Serena and me in 2016. (Age 82)

Hugh and Sanne, 1955 at Cornell before we were
married

Reminiscences, Munich, 1934

I was born in an old age home in Munich, Germany, in November 1934, during the Nazi regime when Hitler was in power and had already begun to marginalize the country's Jews. New legislation prevented Jews from working in many professions, including that of medicine and journalism. Savage gangs of Storm Troopers, the SA run by Ernst Röhm, were free to attack Jews and others on the street or imprisoning people in what was inversely called "protective custody." Soon, the Nazis would even deny Jews German citizenship. The German medical system was socialized, so Jews, who were not considered citizens under the Nuremberg Laws, could not join. My father, Samuel Simche Kalter, MD, was prevented from being paid for his medical appointments because he was a Jew, and therefore not a citizen. He had to subcontract from a non-Jewish doctor's practice. This arrangement worked for a while, but eventually it became too dangerous for his medical colleague to be closely associated with a Jew. Eventually, my father had no way of earning a living as a doctor.

German Law for Professionals During Nazi Times

Hitler came to power on January 30, 1933 despite his party's not getting a majority of votes in the election. Former chancellor Papen and his cohorts supported his being placed in power, as they also joined the government (Papen as Vice-Chancellor) and thought that they could "tame" him. Tragically, they seriously miscalculated their ability to control the Nazi Party.

Soon after the election, the Nazi Party pushed through new laws, which were vigorously (and often violently) enforced. These laws reflected Hitler's racist ideology towards Germany's Jews, who numbered 535,000 out of a general population of 67 million. He included this edict:

"All Jews exercising so-called free vocations as lawyers, physicians, artists, etc. are placed under what is called "exception rules." In plain words, that means that Jewish lawyers are not allowed to plead cases before German law courts, that Jewish doctors have been removed from the staffs of hospitals and cooperative health institutions more or less violently, and the actors and orchestra leaders are no longer permitted to act or lead."

Hitler's Opinion on Education of Germans

The entire education and upbringing of citizens of the state must reach a pinnacle (a crowning achievement) so that a sense and feeling of race is instinctively and intellectually burned into the heart and mind of the youth entrusted to them. There should be no young girl or boy leaving school without having come to an ultimate understanding for the necessity and the intrinsic nature (value) of the purity of German blood.

In this way, a prerequisite for the preservation of racial fundamentals will be established for our nationhood, thus procuring security for the necessities for our cultural evolution.

—Adolf Hitler, The Nuremberg Laws of 1935

JEWS COULD NOT PRACTICE their professions or get education because they did not have "purity of German blood."

My dad found a position at a Jewish Community Old-Age Home (*Jüdisches Altersheim*) in return for a free apartment and board for our family. My Mom became the operations manager for the home, overseeing the intake of patients and supervising the staff and the Kosher kitchen. I was born during their tenure.

Living in The Altersheim

As a young child, my living in the *Altersheim* (Old Age Home) was an unusual experience. I had many "grandparents," mostly women, who indulged me with heaps of attention. Some of the older residents suffered from dementia or exhibited strange behavior, while others were frightening and shared "old wives" tales with me. I remember one particular old lady; she scared me by telling me that picking my nose would lead to worms crawling around in my brain.

Fortunately, most of the old people were kind and loving. Playing in the kitchen was a treat. I was allowed to lick the cookie batter bowls. I can still remember the delicious smells of Challah and the Shabbat desserts being prepared. Sometimes a staff member would get irritated and do something deliberately nasty. One kitchen worker who was particularly exasperated with *Kashrut* routines purposefully switched the dishcloth for *fleishig* (meat) dishes with the dishcloth for the *milchig* (dairy) dishes. My mother noticed what had happened and replaced the dishcloths. Being a very forgiving woman, she did not scold the worker. She just laughed.

My mother's job was to oversee the daily operations of running the home. Although she was not trained for this type of work, she had a natural talent for organizing the staff and for soothing and comforting the residents. No amount of experience could have prepared her for some of the bizarre events that she encountered and the jobs she had to perform. For instance, after an elderly resident died during Mom's very first night at the Home, she notified the appropriate officials. When two attendants arrived to remove the body, they were furious with my mother because she had neglected to straighten out the corpse. Since the deceased lay in a curled position and was in *rigor mortis*, the body could not be loaded on a stretcher. My Mom was mortified and apologized.

A much more serious incident occurred when two residents, both in wheelchairs, became very angry at each other with one pushing the other close to the staircase. The wheelchair rolled down the stairs and the patient fell, was severely injured and died. I watched the entire episode in horror and was told not to mention anything of what I had seen. My father had to write a death certificate, and he reported that the cause of death was an accident. He was concerned that there might be an investigation that would risk closing the Home. Even at the young age of four, I realized that telling authorities what I had seen would cause a serious crisis with very negative outcome for all concerned.

The Old Age Home was funded by the *Jüdische Kultusgemeinde* and was located on *Matildenstrasse* in Munich, not far from the *Frauenkirche*, a beautiful and beloved landmark. We were also close to the Zoo and the Botanical gardens. Munich was a lovely city with a famous opera house, concert halls, art galleries, churches and museums. The city was situated on the Isar River, which offered many boat trips in Bavaria. The Jewish population loved Munich and enjoyed its life, at least before the Nazi era. My grandmother, Betty, lived within walking distance, and my father's sister, Gisela, and her husband, Otto, and their two young daughters, Hannah and Else, also lived close by. Anti-

Semitism was rife but there were many good relationships between non-Jewish and Jewish residents. My mother's closest friend was Paula Lottner, an observant Catholic. While the Nazis were doing everything possible to destroy relations between Jews and the rest of German society, there were still many people who cherished their friendships with their Jewish neighbors.

My Birth Certificate: Geburtsurkunde, Certificate, 1934, Note the Swastika on the seal!

My mother wanted me to be a tomboy, not a sappy girl with curls and pink ribbons. She dressed me in boys' clothes, usually *Lederhosen*, and gave me a boys' haircut. She called me Peterle (little Peter) instead of a girl's name. I am very proud of that. She rarely bought me shoes and believed that I should go barefoot. She chose boy's clothes for me so that I could play comfortably and I was delighted to be able to climb, run and jump like the boys I knew. Even today, I still go barefoot on hikes and am called "The Barefoot Grandma" at my Israeli Folk Dancing club.

Munich was well known for its excellent beer and special brews. There was a low alcohol beer for pregnant women and vitamin rich beer for nursing mothers. My mother told me that I was weaned on beer. I found out that my family name, Kalter, which means "the cold one" came from my father's grandfather who was a brewer and manufactured a tasty cold beer in Poland.

Munich's *Maximillians Universität* had a stellar faculty with Alois Altzheimer, Hans Adolph Krebs, Wilhelm Conrad Roentgen, Konrad Lorenz, Werner Heisenberg, Max von Laue, and many world-famous Nobel laureates and experts in scientific fields. My father received his medical education at the *Maximillians Universität*, with a two-year interruption during the First World War when he was drafted as a medical officer in the Austrian army on the Eastern Front. He resumed his medical education after the end of WWI in 1918. Sadly, Jewish students had extreme difficulties gaining admission to the university.

My Father

My father, Samuel Simche Kalter, was born in Rzeszow, Austria-Hungary (now Poland) to Maier Kalter and Regina (Ryfka) Rager Kalter, in August, 1894. His birth came after the deaths of several infant siblings and he had only one living sister, Gisela. According to Nazi law, he was considered Polish and not a German citizen. He was extremely eccentric, had severely crippled feet, was in constant pain and was a heavy smoker. In 1916 he was drafted into the Austrian Army as a medic, but he was unable to march. Because he was short in stature, when he wore his dress uniform, his long sword clanked with every step he took. He was sent to the Eastern front, which was rather quiet at that time and saw very few injured soldiers. The soldiers in his company found him very strange because he was a Jew and seemed not to be interested in women. One night they decided to play a trick on him. They told him that there was an extremely sick woman in the nearby town who required immediate medical attention. My naive father replied that he was on duty and couldn't leave the base to attend to her. His colleagues persevered, so he finally went to the woman's house. He climbed the stairs and stepped into a dark hallway. After knocking on the door, a partially naked woman let him in. He took out his stethoscope, told her to say "Aahh," thumped her chest, took her temperature and then told her after the examination that she was very healthy. She was completely puzzled and angry. At this point, his colleagues broke in expecting him to be in bed with her. He finally understood that he had been tricked and she wasn't a "patient" after all.

Before Dad took the appointment with the Old Age Home, he allied himself with a non-Jewish doctor who assigned him most of the night calls and various "unpleasant" emergencies. One night he received a call from a patient, whose first name was Jenny, with severe lower intestinal pain. Dad took the streetcar to her apartment with his brand new sigmoidoscopic, gave her an enema, and took a stool sample. He couldn't afford a collection kit for the feces, so he used a matchbox. On his way home, he was pick-pocketed in the streetcar. He returned to take a second sample, an unpleasant experience for the patient as well as for my father but not as unpleasant as for the thief. Dad named his new sigmoidoscopic "Jenny" in honor of its first use.

My Dad in The Austrian Army age 22, around 1916

Registering the Old Age Home

One difficulty my parents experienced was maintaining the registration of the Old Age Home (*Altersheim*). The Nazis required weekly registration for the Home. While the registration office was within in walking distance of the Home, it was impossible to get there legally. According to Nazi laws, Jews were not permitted on the sidewalks and were compelled to walk in the gutters. There was no way to enter the registration office without crossing the sidewalk, and therefore there was no way of obeying both laws. The enforcement of the law was sporadic, but it was a nerve-wracking and caused considerable tension. My parents feared opening the door to see Nazi officials demanding to see the Home's current registration papers. Infractions would not just result in monetary fines. Even small misdemeanors could lead to being dragged off to one of the many SA-run "protective custody" prisons.

Anti-Semitism, 1938

Despite everything my parents went through, my childhood was fairly happy and without incident before 1938. I was insulated from most of the surrounding Anti-Semitism, but felt the stress and tension that my parents were experiencing. Although of their friends and relatives talked of leaving Germany, my Dad was committed to staying and caring for his elderly patients. My Mom was reluctant to leave her mother, *Oma* Betty, and her youngest brother, Paul, who had Down syndrome, and needed Mom's help to care for him and to protect him from the Nazi euthanasia program. Soon after Hitler became Chancellor, the administration legalized the murder of those who they considered unsuitable. "Life unworthy of life" was a horrific new way of looking at those suffering from schizophrenia, and certain hereditary conditions. Only people they considered worthy of being part of the German *"Volk"* (people) were to remain citizens.

Uncle Paul was ineligible for a US visa because of having Down syndrome. The United States did not grant visas for the "feeble minded" and we knew Paul was at risk for *Euthanasie*. Although my parents applied for American visas, they had a very high quota number and thus knew they had a very low chance to receive them.

Since January 1933, when Hitler was named Chancellor by President Paul von Hindenburg, who died in 1934, conditions for German Jews steadily worsened and more and more Anti-Semitic legislation was put into effect. Due to a terror campaign by the SA, the Storm Troopers, and heated rhetoric by Hitler himself and others in the Nazi leadership, many regular Germans, including those in southern Germany (Bavaria) where we lived, embraced his policies. While not everyone agreed with Nazi policy, most became bystanders and were silent to the growing list of atrocities, however many Germans were very enthusiastic supporters of Hitler and his policies. Soon, my parents realized it was time to flee Germany. My mother organized and packed our belongings, paying the furniture movers to load it all into a moving van. She pre-paid the shipping and insurance costs to the USA, in case the visas were granted. As soon as the moving van left, she realized that its contents would probably be stolen before even reaching the next corner and would go straight to the Nazis who were laughing at how neatly everything was packed.

The So-Called "Polenaction" - The Expulsion of Polish Jews From the Reich, 1938/1939

Life became very dangerous for Jews, especially after we were stripped of our German citizenship in 1935. It was especially dangerous for Jews who had immigrated to Germany years before from another country. My father, who was born in 1894 in what was then Austria-Hungary, and only became Poland after new boundaries were drawn in 1918, was now designated as Polish. His citizenship defaulted to that of Poland.

"Hitler spread the idea that Jews had been the enemy from within, proposing that the German Army would have won the war had some of them not been gassed to death." (See *The Death of Democracy* by Benjamin Carter Hett.) President Paul von

Hindenberg spread the lie that the "Army was stabbed in the back by Jews and Socialists" (see *Hitler's Rise To Power* by Benjamin Hett.) These statements, pushed by Goebbels, led to mass deportations of German Jews. Nazis stormtroopers deported my family and me by train, to Poland, on October 27, 1938. We had no time to pack or get organized, and I got separated from my parents shortly after getting on the train. The train ride was long even though the distance to the Polish border was short. There were many stops during which the Nazis (SS) interrogated the deportees. I was questioned by three armed SS officers, who were fishing for names of people whom they believed were hidden in the Old Age Home. They suspected that we were hiding Jews there, and they kept asking me if various people "visited" or "stayed" with us. Fortunately, I did not know to answer their questions nor incriminate anyone. I had no understanding of guns, but I felt the danger nevertheless. I recall my answer, which was *"Mein Name ist Susanne Thekla Kalter, und mehr weiß ich nicht."* (My name is Susanne Thekla Regina Kalter and that is all I know.)

My stubborn rebellious nature, which has lasted me all my life, prevented my giving in to their demands. Those Nazi bullies received no information from me.

The train was stopped at the Polish border, but the Poles did not accept the passengers as Polish citizens. As far as the Poles were concerned, we were German Jews and they didn't want us. They tried to return the train, but the Germans wouldn't allow the train re-enter Germany. We were stuck on the border with no fresh food or water for about a week. The dreadful toilet facilities were in the last carriage on the train, and I was afraid to cross the gaps between carriages, as there was no protection from falling onto the track, just an empty gap with a connector, and I was afraid that I would fall onto the tracks. We were allowed to stand on the platform of the train station but could not leave. One day, after a violent rainstorm, I saw a rainbow and I was convinced that it was a sign that everything would be all right. Finally, there were some negotiations between the Poles and the Germans, and the train was permitted to return to Germany with its Jews.

Another young child, Arno Penzias from Munich, was on the same train. Dr. Penzias, who won the Nobel Prize in Physics in 1978, was six years old when his family was rounded up for deportation to Poland. Arno and his brother were sent to England on the Kindertransport, where his parents eventually rejoined their sons. The family immigrated to the USA in 1940. The Nazis, in their frenzy to get rid of all Jews, destroyed the careers of scientists, artists and authors who could have enriched much the world's culture. Fortunately, the Penzias children were saved through the efforts of the Kindertransport that enabled unaccompanied children to travel to England and Canada.

That was just the beginning of the horror in Germany. The night of November 9th, shortly after our thwarted train ride to Poland, and just before my 4th birthday on November 20th, several SS Stormtroopers crashed through my window into our ground floor apartment in the Old Age Home, breaking all the window glass. This became known as Kristallnacht, "Night of Broken Glass," the pogrom that started in the old city hall in Munich. The Stormtroopers, all holding guns, demanded that I take them to the office where my parents were reviewing patients' charts. They took the keys and locked all of the residents into their rooms and demanded the names, ages and papers of every resident. They took an inventory of the money and valuables in the office and, true to German bureaucracy, gave my mother a receipt for all of the items they stole. We were then transported to Dachau, the very first concentration camp, just a few miles from Munich.

Vehicles, already waiting, transported all of the residents, staff and my family to Dachau that was only seven miles from Munich. Dachau was a work-labor camp in 1938, not yet a death camp, but several of the elderly patients died because they were missing their medications and were unable to work or even walk. The Nazis soon realized that the mass incarceration of the residents of the Old Age Home was a liability, so we were released. The staff was allowed to go back to the Old Age Home with those patients who survived. Their release was accomplished after a financial payment. It was certainly not a good-will action.

My Escape to Holland

Photograph in the Holocaust Museum (Photograph Number: 97264): Tom, Wolf, and Michael Stein play with their maternal grandparents in their home in Amsterdam. (Photo probably taken in 1937)

In desperation, my mother gave me to a wonderful Gentile woman who took the risk of using her deceased daughter's birth documents for me, and smuggled me to Holland. She gave me a sleeping pill so that I wouldn't cry and compromise the escape. One mistake could result in an arrest. We traveled by train to the Dutch border and were met by a scene of drunken border guards who were partying in celebration of the first birthday of Princess Irene, born to Queen Juliana of the Netherlands. The guards were too drunk to check our documents and we were able to cross without incident.

I was placed at first with a Dutch family, who transferred me to a second family, in order to disguise the chain of the escape. I was eventually taken to the Stein family, my mother's relatives, who lived in Amsterdam. According to the account of seven-year-old Tom, the middle Stein child, I arrived stuffed into a suitcase. I don't believe this story, but Tom's version is certainly colorful. After emerging from the suitcase, I asked, in my strong Bavarian accent, where I was and where my parents were. I threatened to jump out of the window if they did not answer my questions. They replied in Dutch rather than in German, and probably did not answer my questions, as their maid, who was present, could have reported my illegal entry into the country. I did not understand Dutch, so my questions were not answered, or so I thought. I didn't want to undermine my bluff, so I jumped out of their window and broke my arm. This was a disaster because I was "illegal," and they could not call a doctor, as that would expose my hiding place.

The Stein family had a summer home in the resort town of Zandfoort, where three Stein boys and I were taken with their nanny, *Yeuffie*, because it seemed safer to be away from Amsterdam where everyone knew the family. The boys were very happy to have a "little sister" and were very kind to me. They included me in their games and even allowed me to join in their favorite competition, "pee up the wall." The kid who peed the highest was the winner. I was thrilled to be accepted by the boys but, to my dismay, I couldn't enter the competition for lack of "parts." What to do? We devised other games in which I could participate, including teasing their poor nanny. We thought that this was hysterically funny and didn't realize how awful she must have felt. My mother had always called me "*Peterle*," or "Little Peter," so I felt quite at home with the boys and loved having three brothers. The Stein parents desperately wanted a girl, and, to my horror, they put a huge pink bow in my hair. It didn't go well with my Lederhosen, but I had to wear it.

My hiding in Zandfoort was pleasant, except that I couldn't go outside for fear of being discovered. The Stein family needed to go on a trip one day. Their car could not hold all of the children, so the youngest, Michael and I, were left behind. We conspired to take revenge on his parents. At my instigation, Michael and I tore up newspapers, got some paste, and completely smeared up the windows and made a huge mess. I was a brat and thoroughly enjoyed making mischief, and I suffered the punishment cheerfully.

I enjoyed having three brothers and completely forgot about my German home, my parents, and even the German language. I had learned to speak Dutch, which is not terribly different from German. Some Dutch were afraid of, and hated, the Germans because of their invasion in WW1, so we were not allowed to speak German. After a while, I was completely assimilated into my new family.

One day a man, whom I did not recognize, arrived at the house and had a hurried conversation with the Stein parents. They packed a suitcase for me and drove us to the port. That man was my father. He had escaped from Germany and possessed tickets for a night ferry to England. We didn't know it then, but we crossed on one of the last Channel crossings before the Germans invaded Holland on May 10, 1940. We traveled from The Hague to Dover, reaching England, just in time. The Stein parents and their oldest son, Wolf, were eventually caught and sent to the concentration Camp, Bergen-Belsen, where Anne Frank later died of typhus. The two younger boys, Tom and Michael, were hidden by Dutch farmers.

My father's sister, Gisela, and her husband, Otto Wolff, had also smuggled their two daughters to Holland. Their older daughter, Hannah, was sent to relatives in 1935 and later was hidden by a Dutch farmer. Their younger daughter, Else, was sent to live with a Christian family in 1939. Otto Wolff, who owned a men's clothing store in Germany, had his business trashed on *Kristallnacht*. Both Gisela and Otto Woolf disappeared in 1940 and have never been heard from again. My father assumed that they were sent to a concentration camp where they were murdered. Hannah and Else were saved from the camps because they were hidden by farmers in the country. They both become nurses after the war. We met the cousins when Hugh and I were in Germany in 1956 and we helped them immigrate to the USA in 1958.

The Netherlands had a large number of Holocaust victims and it is estimated that 75% of Dutch Jews did not survive, which is one of the highest Holocaust death rates in Europe, There were many Jews living in the Netherlands in 1939, among them 24,000 to 25,000 who had fled Germany and Austria. The Nazi occupation force put the number of Dutch Jews in 1941 at 154,000, according to their census. In 1945, only about 35,000 Jews were still alive. In 1947, 14,346 Jews were in the Netherlands. 107,000 Dutch Jews were sent to Westerbork and from there were deported to Sobibor, Bergen-Belsen, Theresienstadt, and Auschwitz, death camps in Poland and Austria. Of these 107,000 Jews, only 5,200 survived. An estimated 16,500 Jews managed to survive the war by hiding in Holland. There were 102,000 Jews who fell victim to the Nazis. Some were native Dutch, and others were refugees who attempted to seek asylum in the Netherlands.

Dutch policemen rounded up Jewish families to be sent to their deaths in Eastern Europe. Trains of the Dutch railways, staffed by Dutch employees, transported the Jews to camps in the Netherlands that were transit points to Auschwitz, Sobibor, and other death camps. "With respect to Dutch collaboration," Eichmann is quoted as saying, "The transports run so smoothly that it is a pleasure to see."

Photo of Dad's Sister, Gisela Kalter Wolff. Copyright ©
2018 Yad Vashem. The World Holocaust
Remembrance Center

Three of my mother's unmarried cousins, Erna, Frieda, and
Kaethe Meyerstein had already escaped to London by 1939.
Their two older sisters, who were married and had children,
were murdered in the Holocaust. After the war, my family
helped the surviving sisters immigrate to the USA.

London

My mother escaped from Germany to England a few weeks before my father and I arrived in London. She established a temporary residence in a shared London flat. She was sponsored by an extraordinarily brave and generous woman, Catherine Lucas, an unmarried young Christian secretary. Catherine lived very frugally on her meager salary but committed herself to support my mother and our family, if necessary. She was ready to house and feed us even if my parents could not find work. Catherine was an angel without whom we could not have survived.

There wasn't enough space for me in the room that my mother had rented, so I was sent to an English boarding school, where I couldn't understand a word anyone said. I didn't know English, or the rules and customs of the school, so I got into trouble immediately. Every schoolgirl had been issued a uniform that had to be kept clean and ironed to enter the dining room. A common practice was for the girls to exchange their dirty uniforms for a clean one from a new girl. I was a target, and I found a filthy uniform on my bed in exchange for my newly issued clean one. I was not allowed to enter the dining room wearing the dirty uniform, and so I had to skip a day of eating and wash and iron the uniform. The next day I was given some "porridge" for breakfast which was slimy, disgusting and foreign, and I couldn't swallow it. I was told to sit there until I finished it, but I didn't understand the command. I sat until lunchtime and the porridge, cold by now, had turned into a glue-like substance. The counselor tried to induce me to eat the stuff by adding sugar to the slimy concoction, which made it even less appealing. I sat there until dinnertime and the staff finally let me go to bed. I was really proud of my stubbornness and vowed that I would never eat oatmeal again.

Boarding School and Hostel

The boarding school was a nightmare, and I begged my mother to let me leave. I had relearned enough German in order to speak with my Mom and Dad. My parents were registered as enemy aliens because Germany was at already war with England, and they were unable work except as domestic servants and in a few other categories for which they were over-qualified. My mother secured a position at a *Kindertransport* hostel, which housed 16 children from a variety of European countries. She scrounged around London to obtain partially used ration cards to buy food for the children. I always admired my mother's amazing ability to do work for which she was not professionally trained. She had no fear about doing any type of task. Mom cooked and cared for the children who were traumatized by being separated from their families as well as living in a country where they couldn't speak the language. There were Dutch, Czech, French, German, Hungarian, Romanian and Polish children who couldn't communicate with each other. It was a Tower of Babel. One girl was so traumatized that she could not eat anything that was red. On the night we were served tomato soup, she ran screaming from the room. A young boy, whom we called "Birdie," used to take baths with his socks on claiming that it would help him dress quickly if an air raid started.

My mother gave some me important advice, the most useful of which was to always be able to support myself. She advised me to choose an occupation that can be useful in any country. Science is universal and jobs are available in every country. Another piece of advice that she gave me, that I misinterpreted, was that I should always be modest. This became an obstacle when I applied for jobs at American companies. I always under-rated myself in my personal evaluation.

Pluto, My Toy

I recall an incident when I became sick and vomited all over a stuffed animal named Pluto. My mother washed Pluto, but he disintegrated in the wash. I felt quite bereft without my "friend." There was a cat in the home that often came and slept in my bed. One morning I felt several lumps in the bed and realized that the mother cat had delivered three kittens under the covers. I was proud that the mother cat had enough trust in me to deliver her kittens in my bed. I have adored cats since then.

The Blitz

We were in London during the Blitz, the German aerial terror bombing of London in 1940 and 1941, which lasted for eight months. London was bombed on 57 consecutive nights, as well as in the daytime. Much of that time was spent in our air raid shelter under the house basement. More than 13,000 civilians were killed, and almost 20,000 injured, during September and October alone. The Blitz claimed about 40,000 lives from the air raids and possibly more. When the sirens began to wail, we ran down to the shelter before it got locked. We were issued gas masks and had only a bucket for a toilet. Gas for cooking and heating was turned off in the event order to prevent fires in the event that we were hit by bombs, so we shivered all during that cold and damp winter. The older children amused the younger ones by sharing stories and singing until the "all clear" sirens were heard. This went on for hours every night for several months. The worst night was when 600 people were killed In September, 1940, when a German bomb fell on Hallsville Junior School, burying alive the 600 civilians sheltering in its basement. Over a million homes were hit or destroyed by the Luftwaffe. I still get goosebumps when I hear fire or police sirens. It was terrifying.

The most difficult times were when sirens went off on my way home from my new school. There often wasn't enough time to get home, so I had to duck into the Underground (the subway system) for safety. Thousands of people were on the underground station platforms waiting for the raid to end. There were neither food nor adequate toilet facilities for such a large number of people. When we emerged from the Underground, we were met with the sight of burning houses and rubble. I always ran all the way home so my parents knew I hadn't perished in the bombing. By May 1941, the threat of a German invasion receded, so things were calmer.

Coming to South Wales

The government ministries in London decided that schools needed to be closed and that children were to be sent to the countryside, which was considered to be safe from bombings, although not from a German invasion. My parents and I were sent to South Wales to a coal mining town in Carmarthenshire-a long distance from London. Wales did not consider German Jewish refugees to be "enemy aliens," so my father was able to procure a position in a hospital for infectious diseases in Carmarthenshire. The local doctor had been drafted into the British army, so my father became the interim doctor for the coal town of Upper Tumble and was a chief of service at the Carmarthenshire Hospital. We lived in a staff cottage at the hospital that was located several miles out of town, so that the townspeople would be safe from infection.

Antibiotics were unavailable for civilians during the war because all penicillin supplies were requisitioned by the armed forces. My father treated his patients with sulfa drugs and old-fashioned treatments for miners' diseases that included, black lung disease, pneumonia and tuberculosis. He was an excellent physician, proud that he was able to save most of his patients.

Soon he became a local hero. The local Baptist clergyman, Minister Williams, his wife, and the mine owner, with whom we became great friends, warmly welcomed our family into the community. Our family was invited to join the Baptist Church in Upper Tumble, and we enjoyed the beautiful music in the church, especially the Christmas concerts. It would have been rude of our family to refuse to join the church that welcomed us so warmly and there was no pressure to convert. The congregants were puzzled about what Jews were, as we were the first Jews to live in Tumble.

I attended the local school in Llanelly (no-one can pronounce the name correctly except for natives) and I seemed to fit in quite well. I learned Welsh and was soon able to understand the school subjects. On my first day, the other children felt my forehead and rubbed it back and forth. I had no idea what was happening until Minister Williams explained that the local people thought that Jews had horns. The children believed that I had them shaved off and that they would be able to feel the stumps.

Living in Wales

There were great advantages to living in the country in Wales. Most importantly it was spared, for the most part, from German air raids. The local mining families often had small farms, so we were often presented with fresh food. We had access to milk, eggs, cheese, berries and apples, items that were unavailable in stores. Another advantage to my living in Wales was riding the miners' bus to school (which was near the Upper Tumble mine) and listening to the miners sing four-part *a cappella* Bach cantatas. Their voices were marvelous, and I enjoyed the daily bus concerts that were on *par* with the best concerts in London. School children had daily singing classes, and my voice was no match for the lovely voices of the other children. I was too ashamed to sing, so I just pretended and "mouthed" along.

School was difficult for me, because I was considered privileged by being "the doctor's daughter." The custom was that everyone was caned (hit by a stick) upon entering and leaving school; the girls on the palm and the boys on the back of the hand, that was much more painful. The idea behind the first caning, in the morning, was a warning against being bad during the day, and the second caning was for infractions that the

27

teacher missed seeing during the school day. I was spared the caning because of my status, and the other students were resentful. One day I rode my bike to school (no-one else had a bike), and the kids all asked me to let them have a ride during recess. Because of all of the rides I gave, I was late coming in from recess, and the teacher felt she had to cane me. The boys got caned based on a schedule of infractions, but the girls only got caned until they cried, usually after one strike. I made sure that I would NEVER cry, which only made the teacher angrier and angrier. As a result I got struck many times. The kids were amazed to see me so stoic, and I never had any trouble with them after that.

One of the students made me furious when she made an extremely anti-Semitic remark so I wanted to thrash her. The kids all yelled, "Fight, Fight!" She was much bigger than I was so it was a hopeless match. I gave it my best but I lost the fight and was humiliated. I learned that I should never fight a bigger person. This has served me well later on, because I never achieved a height of five feet, and thus would never be able to win a physical fight.

The town of Upper Tumble, in the Gwendraeth Valley, had an anthracite mine (very hard and smokeless coal) and the only jobs in Tumble were at the mine, the post office, grocery store, school and church. The mine was extremely deep, and there were three levels of elevators to get to the deepest coal tunnels. There was a huge slag hill near the mine and I feared that it would slip and bury me. I was allowed to take the elevator down into the mine because my Dad had become friends with the mine manager, but I was so claustrophobic that I wanted to come up after I reached the first level. I had to wait a long time until the all miners were delivered to their lowest destination, abut 300 feet, and the elevator was free to return to the surface. It was a terrifying experience, but I was lucky to have had it since I was probably the only child to deeply descend into a coal mine except for the children who had worked in the mines decades before.

I became good friends with the mine manager's daughter, Anne Davis-Jones, and joined a group of her friends. We cycled around the countryside or played "hide-and-seek" in a huge barn full of busses that were grounded because there was no fuel during the war. It was impossible to find the "hiding child" because there were many busses, and we could silently creep from one to another bus unseen. It was the very best game I ever played. Most of the time we jumped rope or played hop-scotch when we could not locate the key that gave us access to the bus barn.

There were many shortages during the war, especially imported goods. But most of the shortages didn't affect me directly. There was one exception that I remember very clearly. Because of the scarcity of rubber that was needed for tanks and airplanes for the British forces, my mother gave me a very bouncy rubber ball for my birthday. There was very little rubber available for civilians, and bike tires were endlessly re-patched because it was impossible to buy new ones. My mother saved coupons for months and finally had enough to buy a ball. I was thrilled to have the ball, and I went out to play with the magi-cally bouncy object. One big bounce took the ball straight into a hedge with a field on the other side. I frantically searched for it until sunset, finally going home to admit what had happened. My mother's reaction surprised me. She had thought something horrible had happened to me and her relief and fear were so overwhelming upon my arrival that she slapped me. At the time, I felt this was very unfair. But now that I have had children of my own, I understand how terrified she had been for several hours. I never found the ball and I felt that its loss was punish-ment enough.

Petrol (gasoline) was rationed, so I was never able to travel and see the country. I had the opportunity to go to the beach town of Mumbles and I took a bus trip to Cardiff. The country-side was beautiful and I saw some fascinating mediaeval castles. Despite the invariably bad weather I enjoyed these trips. I found plenty of opportunities to have fun in the little town, Upper

Tumble. The best times were at the "Magic Lantern" shows, which were held at the church on a weekly basis. One of the movies I saw was "Madame Curie," and I was immediately inspired to become a scientist. I never deviated from that dream, and I later got my wish by going to The Bronx High School of Science in New York, City College of New York, Cornell University, and the University of California, at Berkeley for my graduate work in microbiology. I am so happy that I was able to see the movie that inspired my lifelong dream.

Photo of Mom and me in Wales, (circa 1944)

The thing that dominates my memories of Wales was the fear my parents had for their relatives left behind in Germany. My father never received any letters from his sister Gisela. and her family, the Wolffs, but my mother did receive heavily censored letters from her mother, my Oma (Grandma Betty Katzenstein) and from her non-Jewish best friend, Paula Lottner. My Oma's letters stopped suddenly, and the silence was torture. Eventually Mom's friend, Paula, wrote that Oma Betty and her two sons had been "taken away." This was terrible news as we had heard rumors that Jews were being killed in concentration camps. After the war, we found out that that Oma Betty, aged 75, and her sons, Paul and Jacob, were deported to *Theresienstadt* (Terezin) near Prague, and eventually to Auschwitz where they were murdered.

Oma Betty's work assignment at camp was to wash the socks of the SS officers, a sickening and stinking job. She became ill hauling the water for the laundry. Her disabled son, Paul, was probably gassed immediately. We never found out what exactly happened to Robert (Bob), but he did not survive the camp. My father's sister, Gisela, and her husband, Otto Wolff, were never heard from again. Their two daughters, Hannah and Else, survived in Holland.

The Hospital in Carmarthenshire

My father worked hard to care for his patients in the Carmarthenshire hospital, and often made home visits to patients in the surrounding country and farms. The hospital collected the ration cards of the incoming patients and used them in the hospital commissary kitchen to buy food for them. Many of the patients were too ill to eat, so there was always left-over food that supplemented the diets of the staff, including my family. My father had been trained in Internal Medicine, but he occasionally had to attend obstetrical patients when the Ob-Gyn specialist was unavailable. On one occasion, he had an obstetrical patient who was just about to deliver her baby, but since Dad had just been in the infectious disease ward he felt uncomfortable about taking care of her. There was another medical officer on duty, so my father went on the intercom and called, for everyone to hear, "Would Dr. Jones please come to the maternity section, because you are the only sterile man around." Of course, everyone who heard the announcement laughed, and my father had no clue that he had said something completely outrageous in English.

My favorite occupation was to spend time in the hospital

kitchen and watch the cooking personnel at work. The item that fascinated me the most was the potato peeler. I was amazed and excited by the machine, which looked like a washing machine with sandpaper lining the barrel. The potatoes bounced around while the machine whirled, and they were thoroughly peeled in a couple of minutes. The kitchen workers were kind and tolerant of me, and I spent a great deal of time there learning Welsh conversation and songs.

A new student appeared at the Llechyfedach School one day, and the teacher explained to us that she was the daughter of an American soldier who was stationed nearby. What was unusual about the young girl was that she was brown-skinned, then called "Negro," and none of us had ever seen a Negro before. I felt very sorry for her because she couldn't speak Welsh, so I befriended her. Unfortunately, I cannot remember her name and have no idea where she might be living after the war. I had never heard of prejudice against Negroes (Blacks) and this was the very first Negro I had ever met. Her father was reassigned, and the family moved away. I am surprised that a black American soldier had been able to bring his family to England.

My time in Wales was pleasant and I enjoyed the farmers, miners and other residents very much. I remember becoming superstitious for a brief time after hearing a folk tale that suggested that people who stepped on cracks would get broken backs, so I avoided that danger for a long time. I can't believe that I could have believed such nonsense, and that experience cured me from ever harboring superstitions in the future. I was also growing into adolescence and had a crush on one of the male teachers whose first name was Tommy. I wrote his name over and over again in one of my textbooks and, when I was discovered, I had to stay after school for an hour each day for a week.

My Mom kept busy helping the town's women knit scarves, socks and mittens for the soldiers in the armed forces and helping with raffle sales to make money to make gift packages for the military. She was well liked by the people in the town.

My Dad was extremely occupied with his work in the hospital and his house calls to patients who could not travel to see him. This was time consuming as he had no car and had to travel by bus. When he had time in the evenings he would tell me bedtime stories in German. He had a very short repertoire so I heard the same stories over and over again. Still I loved hearing them. It was the nicest thing that he ever did for me. It also helped me retain my German.

I had a terrible experience with an acquaintance of my parents who was in the U.S. army and was stationed nearby. My mother welcomed him with her usual warm hospitality and offered him my room to sleep in. My room had only one bed and I was expected to share it with the American visitor. That night I woke horrified. He was crawling all over me with a hard "thing" poking me. I had no idea what was happening, and I was terribly scared. I didn't tell my parents because I was too shocked and embarrassed, so I slept on the floor for the next few nights. I doubt that today's parents would have been so naive. I never told them about it but I should have. Thankfully there is a different atmosphere today and girls can report sexual molestations. I probably still wouldn't do so, because I would be too embarrassed and I'd feel that I wouldn't be believed.

My first experience with a deadly disease was when my parents told me about a nine-year-old girl who was hospitalized with polio in Llanelly. My parents said that she was lonely and needed visitors, so I took the bus to Llanelly and visited the ward where the young girl was incased in an iron lung. Only her head, reflected in a mirror, was visible. The poor girl had paralytic polio and could not talk. I was terrified at the sight and the realization that she would have to live the rest of her life in that iron lung. We couldn't have a conversation, so I read books to her. I did this once a week for a few times, but then I told my parents it was too terrifying and that I couldn't do it anymore. I still feel ashamed of myself for not having the courage to visit her more often.

Ship to America: Crossing The Atlantic

Late in 1944 it appeared that Germany would lose the war, and my parents believed that my father would lose his position at the hospital as soon as the regular doctor was discharged from the army. Once again, my mother organized and packed all of our belongings and wrote to her two brothers who lived in America, asking them to sponsor our immigration to the USA. As soon as we received our visas, my mother booked tickets for a ship crossing the Atlantic. At that time, there were no passenger ships that crossed the Atlantic, because of the German U-boats and the mines in the North Atlantic. The only ships making the crossing were troop and cargo ships that brought soldiers to Europe and then returned to North America, empty. The departure dates and times were military secrets, so passengers were not notified more than one day before the sailing date. We were on the waiting list for a passage but the family who was on the waiting list ahead of us was not ready to leave. My mother said "Hurry! Ready or not, we are going!" We took a train to Liverpool and embarked that day on the S.S. *Cavina*, a troop ship. Tragically, the ship hit a mine at a later crossing and sank. I wonder what happened to the family whose place we had taken, and whether they were rescheduled for this trip.

The trip across the Atlantic in mid-winter was very slow, and there was nothing to amuse us. The S.S. *Cavina* sailed in a convoy, so she could not travel any faster than the slowest ship. She left Liverpool on December 18, 1944 and arrived in Halifax, Nova Scotia, during the first week in January, 1945. The convoy travelled alternately north and south, and spent New Year's day near the Canary Islands, off the coast of Africa. Watching the rows of ships bobbing up and down made me horribly seasick, so I went below deck. The Cavina, a cargo ship, was not well equipped for passengers, and the dining room and the toilet facilities were awful. I got terribly seasick during the winter storms and going to the mess hall was unappealing. One of the items on the menu was "Grape Nut Flakes." I imagined that they were something to do with grapes and was terribly disappointed when it turned out to be a dry and tasteless cereal. The food was edible but boring; but that didn't matter much, as I was seasick most of the time. The winter storms in the Atlantic were fierce and our little seven thousand-ton ship bobbed and rolled. When I went on the deck the sight of the many columns of ships in the 120-ship convoy rolling around and going up and down, it made me hang over the rail to vomit.

Seeing land again was unbelievably wonderful, and I stumbled and weaved around like a drunken sailor after leaving the ship. We were all examined medically to see if we were fit to enter Canada. My father had hepatitis and was so weak that he could barely walk, making us afraid that we could be denied entry. One part of the examination was a search for weapons. I was surprised and childishly proud that they thought I had a gun at such a young age.

After passing our medical entry exam, we boarded a train station and boarded a train to the United States. At the U.S. border, we were examined again, and at last we were on our way to our destination…New York City. Our arrival was amazing. We were finally in the United States where I looked forward to seeing "colored people," drinking sodas and eating banana splits. I was extremely disappointed to find that "colored people" weren't purple or green but just brown, a shade darker than I am, and I wondered why they were called "colored." Sodas were a disappointment as well, but I liked banana splits.

My mother's brother, Ernst Katzenstein, and his wife, Marlise met us at the station and invited us to stay in their studio apartment in Manhattan until my mother found a room nearby. Uncle Ernst and Aunt Marlise had been shipboard sweethearts. They met in the late '30s, on a voyage from France to America. My aunt and uncle were extremely welcoming, and my mother was overjoyed to see her younger brother again. My parents tried to telephone my uncle Max, Mom's eldest brother, who lived in San Francisco with his wife. The phone reunion was tearful and emotional. Uncle Max had married Aunt Rosl in Germany and I was the flower girl at the wedding. Max had a shoe sales business with the Knapp mail order company and he and Aunt Rosl settled in San Francisco. Aunt Rosl at first worked as a domestic servant with a wealthy family, but later became an accountant, which was her original profession. The couple decided that the name Katzenstein was too difficult and foreign, so they abbreviated it to Katen for business reasons.

The First Weeks In New York

My parents filed their "First Papers" the day after arriving in the United States, the first step for their citizenship application. They were determined to become citizens as soon as possible and to assimilate into the "*Goldene Medina,*" the golden land. They signed up for English lessons and did their best to find lodging, which was a difficult as there were no apartments available at our price range, which was next to zero, since neither of them had jobs. Wartime England would not allow travelers to take more than the currency equivalent of ten dollars per person out of England, so my parents had only $30 to find a place to rent. Until we received our citizenship papers, five years later, and even afterwards, my parents were constantly afraid of being deported. My Mom soon found a job as a house cleaner, but my Dad had a difficult time because he did not have a New York State medical license. After one year he was granted a temporary "Emergency License" by using his medical diploma from Munich, and was able to work night shifts at a hospital for indigent patients. The hospital was located on Welfare Island and, despite his degree, he received minimal pay.

Living in NYC

My mother located a room in a shared apartment in Manhattan, several blocks from my Uncle and Aunt. The apartment had five rooms, some occupied by entire families. There was no corridor in the apartment and this was what was called a "railroad apartment," one had to go through each room to reach the next one. Renters in the front rooms had to endure the occupants of the rear rooms going through their rooms, day or night. There was no privacy. There was a shared kitchen and toilet, but no real bathroom. The kitchen had been remodeled from a bathroom and the kitchen "table" was simply a door placed over the bathtub. We had to sign up for baths (only one per week permitted) and for meals. The single toilet was always occupied. There was no refrigerator, but we had an "icebox" into which a block of ice was delivered each day by a man with a horse and cart. The ice melted into a drip pan and it was my job to empty the pan so that it would not overflow. No-one else bothered. The pan attracted cockroaches that swarmed out whenever I emptied the drip pan.

A single young man occupied the room just beyond our room and, as my parents were out most evenings at their jobs, he would come into our room and crawl into bed with me. It was horrendous. He was usually drunk, smelled bad, and would start molesting me. After kicking and biting him I would get up and sleep on the floor, but he seemed to be too drunk to notice. Fortunately, he was evicted by the manager because of his drinking and so I didn't have to put up with him any longer. I never told my parents because, in the old style of thinking, they were sure to blame me. Anyhow, I was too embarrassed and shaken by the incidents to tell them. Today I might have called the police. Then, of course, we didn't even have a phone.

The apartment manager was a horrible woman named Mrs. Traurig ("sadness" in German) and her personality matched her name. The building was on 77th Street in Manhattan near the beautiful Hudson River, but the apartment was horrible, full of mice and cockroaches. We didn't turn on the light when we entered our room, to avoid warning the roaches of our approach. My Mom and I stomped around crunching the roaches until we had crushed dozens in our little dance. After that we turned on the light, swept away the carcasses and wiped up the crushed cockroach paste. I still remember how was disgusting it was.

School in NYC

I registered for school in January, 1945, and was given a placement test to determine my grade level. I was familiar with pounds, kilograms, sovereigns, farthings, pence, half crowns, furlongs, meters, square meters and all of the British weights and measures, but I couldn't do the math problems because they were in the American system of weights and measures. In addition, I didn't really understand American English very well, as I had been taught in Welsh. My strategy was to boycott the exam rather than receive a poor score. I believed that the examiners would understand that I was not an English speaker and would ignore my test score, however my strategy didn't work. I was designated "retarded," the term used at the time, and placed in a classroom for "special" children. There was fire drill during the first week, and I did what I would have done in London—I ducked under my desk, which was the wrong thing to do in the U.S. I finally noticed that the other children were lined up in the corridor, so I tried to join the line. Since the other students knew their places in the line and wouldn't allow me in, I tried to ask where I should stand. My speaking broke the first rule of fire drills, which was to be silent. I was punished for talking and not standing in line.

I told my parents that I would never go back to that school again. They supported my decision. I spent my days listening to radio stations WQXR and WNYC that had wonderful announcers. I memorized the hourly newscasts that were delivered in perfect and beautiful English. Within a short time, I was able to speak along with the newscasters who repeated the news every hour. I mimicked each broadcast and quickly acquired English with an American accent.

My Move to Malden

My parents sent me to live with my mother's brother-in-law, Dr. Karl Rothschild, and his second wife, Aunt Hennie (Henrietta) who lived in Malden, Massachusetts. Uncle Karl's first wife was my mother's older sister, Thekla, who died of bacterial endo-carditis and had left three young children, my cousins Max, Hannah and Eva. I was sent to Malden, where Uncle Karl was a medical doctor. He had managed to immigrate to America with his wife and his two daughters shortly before the war, and received his Massachusetts medical license after a stint of dish washing at a hospital.

After he discovered that a number of his former German patients lived in the area, Uncle Karl started a medical practice with many of his former patients from Germany. They were delighted to be able to speak in German with him and go to a doctor who understood them. These patients referred other immigrants, and he soon had a booming practice. One of his patients was young Henry Kissinger and his family who had recently immigrated to America.

The waiting room of his practice was a bedroom that was occupied by my cousin, Hannah, who had to get up early to hide the bed and add some chairs every morning, to convert her bedroom into a waiting room. I shared a bedroom with my cousin Eva, who became a sister to me. My cousins came to England on the *Kindertransport* had been reunited their parents in London, and the family came to the United States just before it entered the European war.

Aunt Hennie was the medical receptionist for my uncle and ran his lab tests, billed patients and made appointments. She also had a business sewing fancy opera gloves with sequins and frills. Hennie was a marvelous seamstress and ran a good business. She was an accomplished pianist and singer but didn't have much time to pursue her love of music.

Hennie and Karl were observant Orthodox Jews who adhered strongly to *Halacha*, the Jewish law, of which I knew nothing. It was virtually impossible to practice Judaism or get *Kosher* food in Europe, and there were no synagogues where we lived in Wales. It was always best to keep our Jewishness in low profile, so I was hardly aware of Jewish traditions. Uncle Karl and Aunt Hennie were shocked at my ignorance, and they immediately registered me at the local Orthodox Hebrew School. Not surprisingly, the other students were far ahead of me. The teachers weren't helpful but I managed to catch up fairly quickly. I was amazed to find out that the Germans wanted to annihilate all of the Jews in the world. I had no knowledge about the slander against Jews that had been going on since the Middle Ages in Europe. These things were not discussed at home because it was too frightening.

Malden Schools

The local Catholic parochial school went up to the 5th grade, and then the students were then funneled into the public school system. I felt that many of them were jealous of me as I received superior grades in most subjects. They called me "Banana Nose" and "Christ Killer" and tormented me in the schoolyard. The taunt "Banana Nose" has stayed me throughout my life and caused me to hate the way I look. To this day, I am still embarrassed by the size of my nose. There was a gang of boys led by a bully named Whitey. To humiliate me, he forced me to walk between two lines of his gang members who would then urinate on me and then they tore up my Hebrew school homework. I walked to Hebrew school very slowly to allow my dress the time to dry, and always arrived late. I was chastised for being late and not having my homework. When I tried to explain the reason for my tardiness the response was "Now you know what it is like to be a Jew!" I was furious because these teachers had been living safely in America while I was in danger in Hitler's Europe. What did they know about being a Jew?

I tried to tell my public school teacher about the bullying in the schoolyard and she told me that I had to "learn how to deal with it," however she never taught me how to do that. I never told Uncle Karl and Aunt Hennie about all of the painful things I experienced because they had their own problems, both financial and as immigrants. They wouldn't have known what to do about it anyhow. I didn't know it at the time, but they were desperately worried about Uncle Karl's son, Max, who had been hidden in Holland and hadn't been heard from in years.

I had a difficult time making friends in school because I was different and an outsider. I managed to make friends with three other rejects, and that helped. One day one of the popular girls invited me to her home along with her best friends. I was excited by the invitation because I desperately wanted to belong, but the visit turned out to be a catastrophe. The girls crowded around me and took down my pants because they wanted to know if Jewish girls were circumcised as were the Jewish boys. I didn't know what they were talking about, but I had the misfortune to have my menstrual period at the time and the girls teased me about it. It turned out that I was about two years ahead of the average age for starting menses, and none of the other girls had experienced it. I was humiliated and angry that I had fallen into the trap of thinking that the girls had genuinely sought my friendship. Their brutal cruelty was devastating. I can still feel the humiliation and shame that the experience caused me. Naturally I did not tell anyone.

We weren't allowed to use the phone on Shabbat, but my uncle's phone was essential for his medical practice. We put a towel over the phone so that the ring could not be heard by the observant Orthodox family who lived upstairs. The muffled ring was so faint that one had to sit next to it to hear the ring, so we all took turns phone-sitting. One Saturday, during my turn, there was a long-distance call that Uncle Karl's son, Max, who was alive and had been found in Holland. I ran to tell my aunt and uncle and aunt, but they were so shocked that they slapped me and told me to not play such a dirty trick on them. A few minutes later the phone rang again, and it was Max himself telling Uncle Karl that he was alive and well. Their happiness was unbelievable, and Uncle Karl and Aunt Hennie were both crying. They never apologized for hitting me, but I forgave them because they had been so upset.

My Three Friends

I made friends with three girls in my school. They were all outcasts like me, but I found them to be smart and kind. One of the girls ran home after school every afternoon in order to take care of her bedridden grandmother while her parents were at work. She had to bedpan, feed, wash and take care of her Granny who was very debilitated, so she had little time to play or socialize. She did her homework after her parents came home. My closest friend was the youngest of six siblings whose mother had died of cancer. The oldest sister was in charge of taking care of the younger children and of running the household. Their father was nice but worked hard all day and on weekends, so he could not take care of the children. My friend was very nice but was a bit lost and already had a boyfriend early in her life. She became pregnant and had to drop out of high school. My third girlfriend, the child of divorced parents, was a lovely girl, very shy but friendly. I loved visiting her after school on days when I did not have Hebrew School.

There were a few Jewish kids in my school, and I remember two of them—Michael, on whom I had a huge crush, and a very pretty girl named Marilyn. We spent time together during the Christmas holidays to get strength from each other when we were upset by having to sing Christmas Carols and have speaking parts in Christmas plays. It was very hard to refrain from participating in these activities because of the intense pressure from the school to observe Christmas. The three of us felt that we would surely be punished if there were an "afterlife" because of our participation in the Christian celebrations.

The Melting Pot

This was the era of the "Melting Pot" concept against which I rebelled vigorously because I didn't want to lose my Jewish identity. All of the students were forced to participate in a play called "The Melting Pot" and were given short speeches to recite. We had to drop the written speeches into the melting pot and stir and when I refused to recite my part or drop my paper into the pot and I was punished for my rebellion. I would have preferred the term "cultural mosaic."

I heard about the death of President Franklin Roosevelt on the radio on April 12, 1945, and ran to tell my aunt Hennie. She was shocked at my report and felt that I had misinterpreted what had been reported on the news. Most of the Jewish community was devastated but some were aware of the fact that President Roosevelt was not helpful in allowing Jews to get visas to immigrate to the USA.

Girl Scouts in Malden

The nicest time in Malden was during my stint in the Girl Scouts. My uncle and aunt weren't enthusiastic about my joining the scouts because they felt that the uniforms reminded them of the Hitler Youth, and I agreed with them. But still, I enjoyed being with my troop. We participated in a dance concert at the Boston Garden with the Boston Philharmonic. Our dance was very simple, just running across the Garden in long pastel-colored skirts to Beethoven's 6th symphony, the *Pastoral*. It was wonderful, exciting and absolutely one of the best experiences of my life up to then.

The most awkward activity as a Girl Scout was collecting money for charities in December. I was enthusiastic and won first prize by collecting more money than the other scouts, but was shocked to discover that the money went for Christmas decorations and a Creche scene. How could a nice Jewish girl do a thing like that? I had no idea for what I had been collecting money and, after I won the award, I dropped out of my troop.

My Cousins in Malden

I became Americanized during my time in Malden and felt comfortable with what was expected of me. I shared a room with my cousin, Eva, who was five years older. Eva, and her older sister, Hannah, were already thoroughly Americanized. Eva was in high school, and was wild, rebellious and already had boyfriends. Hannah commuted to Boston University to study engineering, and had a part time job teaching in Hebrew School, so I didn't have very much contact with her. I became fast friends with Eva, who was artistic and musical and lots of fun. She enjoyed having a younger sister and treated me with respect and kindness. I had a boyfriend, but I didn't recognize the relationship for what it was. He came to our house almost daily on some excuse or another, and it totally puzzled me. He was just a lonely kid—an outsider like me. We sometimes went on bike rides together or did homework.

Move Back to NYC

After two years in Malden I moved back in with my parents, because my father had received an "emergency" medical license and found a job at a public hospital on Welfare Island that treated indigent terminal cancer patients. While the work was emotionally stressful and physically exhausting, it brought a little income so that my parents were able to upgrade their living arrangement to a slightly better, but still shared, apartment. Ironically, the name of the new landlady was Mrs. Freulich (happiness, in German) and she was a step up from the previous landlady, Mrs. Traurig (sadness). Our new place had more light, was slightly larger and closer to the back so at least we didn't have the annoyance of the other renters walking through our room.

My Mother's Job

My Mom learned how to do Swedish massage from her cousin, Rose Joseph, who had immigrated from Germany with her young daughter several years before. Mom found a job at

MacLevi's, a "reducing salon" where women went to lose weight. The clients took a mild exercise class, followed by a steam bath and massage. My mother was expected to give seven massages, followed by a half hour break, before giving another set of seven massages. Her break was frequently filled with another client, so she had to complete 15 massages without a bathroom or lunch break. My mother complained to the management and was fired immediately. This experience helped me understand the need for labor unions. She tried to find a job at another MacLevi salon but found out that she had been blacklisted. She followed newspaper ads to look for a new posi-tion and found a job listing in a part of the city that she did not know, and promptly got lost. In desperation, she asked a policeman to guide her to the address and his response was "You don't want to go there, lady!"

My Mom was a short, chubby 55-year-old with her gray hair pulled back in a bun, and she soon found out why the cop didn't want her to go to that address. The job was in a "massage parlor" with the "Johns" lounging in the lobby. Naturally she left in a big hurry. When she told us about the experience we all had a big laugh, even though it must have been unpleasant and embarrassing for her. She eventually found another Swedish massage job in a legitimate establishment.

My Horrible Junior High School

My district junior high school was named "Joan of Arc Jr. High School" that I thought was awful! Girls were forced to take ghastly courses like home economics, cooking and "apartment," while the boys took great courses like mechanical drawing and machine shop. Home Ec. courses featured classes in cooking where we made toast and cocoa over and over again. The entire cooking course covered only the menu of a "typical" breakfast. The "apartment" course was a complete waste of time. We learned how to make a bed and how to change vacuum bags. I had already been doing the cooking and cleaning at home for a long time, so this class was an insult. I was on the academic track, so I wasn't allowed to take typing (in the secretarial track) that would have been useful for college. It never occurred to the teachers that we might have to type term papers in college. Most of the classes were vapid and the contents were boring. I had to take a class called "art weaving" which was also total waste of time. My ancient history class consisted of making clay models of pyramids. I couldn't tell my civics class from my physics class because the content was indistinguishable. The "library" class consisted entirely of filling out "Delaney Cards" but we never were allowed to take out books. I loathed the teacher, who eventually became ill and never returned from her sick leave. After the teacher died, I felt that I had contributed to her death by hating her and felt very guilty.

I had two excellent teachers. One was an African American English teacher who introduced me to literature and grammar, and I owe her enormous debt of gratitude. The other teacher, whose name I remember to this day—Christopher Vaghts— taught a science course and encouraged me to consider going to go to a special high school named Bronx High School of Science. He noted that I had received a perfect score on a test on the Solar System (as I write this, tomorrow is the great Eclipse of 2017) that the rest of the students had all failed. I was proud of his assessment, and I decided to try to go to this marvelous high school. Admission to the Bronx High School required a recommendation from the homeroom teacher and passing a difficult entrance exam. As my homeroom teacher, Mrs. Gould, disliked me, she did not recommend me for the entrance test. I skipped school on the appointed day to go the Bronx High School to take the entrance test anyway. I did not tell my parents because they would have discouraged me from skipping school, but I was determined. The list of applicants did not include my name because, of course, Mrs. Gould didn't recommend me (may she choke to death). I begged the administrator to allow me take the test anyhow. He proposed that if there were a "no show" I could take the test. There were only enough exams for the number of recommended students, but since one student did not show up I was able to take the test. When the names of the successful students were announced in the homeroom, on the intercom, Mrs. Gould said to me "I always knew that you pass it." What a hypocrite! I found out that Mrs. Gould had a perfect record of having her students pass the test and she achieved that goal by recommending only her best students and by discouraging students whom she felt might fail the test.

My Library Catastrophe

My parents were always afraid we could be deported at any moment and were very careful to obey every law. Our documents were completely legal but they worried nevertheless. They warned me to avoid demonstrations and parties in "Greenwich Village" that were full of leftists, folk singers and hot political discussions. Naturally, I gravitated to these places but was always afraid that my parents might find out.

I almost got into serious trouble. I had a summer job as a "counselor in training" at a summer camp and had checked out four books from the public library to take along to read during my free time. The library had a program to check out books for a month, rather than the usual 14 days, and I wanted to take advantage of this plan. I must have made a mistake in filling out the special form, so overdue notices started to arrive at home after two weeks. My parents didn't forward the notices to me, so when I returned from camp I discovered that the books were overdue. I ran to the library to return the books and I learned that I owed a great deal of money that I did not have. I was so anxious that we would be deported that I threw the books on the librarian's desk and ran out. It was such a terrifying experience that I have never returned to a public library again. We were not deported, and I had completely overreacted. Later, I had my husband take our kids to the library to obtain their library cards. I simply couldn't face another librarian.

My Hangouts

My favorite place was the Ethical Culture Society. The Society sponsored youth groups featuring lectures and discussions. My parents had no idea what the Society was all about and were unaware that most of the participants were atheists. I felt comfortable in the non-judgmental environment, and enjoyed meeting the other young people who attended. My other hangout was the Junior Astronomy Club at the Hayden Planetarium that was within walking distance of our apartment. The planetarium had lectures and star shows and even some telescope nights for observing the sky when the weather was clear enough. I developed a keen interest in astronomy and stellar evolution and made a few earthly friends. I also enjoyed the Frick art gallery where I could see some of the finest paintings in the world.

The "Village" and Deportations

My parents warned me not to go to Greenwich Village, but I loved spending time there. The folk-singing craze had just started and artists like Pete Seeger frequently gave concerts. The young people at the Village parties were lively and socially conscious and we had many political conversations and debates. I kept the knowledge of going to these evenings a secret from my parents because they would have been outraged at my behavior. They would have been concerned about a possible deportation because many of the people I associated with were leftists or Communists.

Bronx Science High School

The Bronx High School of Science was wonderful. The faculty was stellar and equivalent to university faculty, and it had high expectations of the students. We were required to take five years of science: one year of physics, chemistry and biology, and then a second year of two of those sciences. We were also required to study two languages (I cheated by taking German for one of them) and five years of math. The math teacher, Dr. Alcalay, was exceptional; he made everyone excited about the subject. Foolishly, I thought that I was good in math but I soon found out I that wasn't talented enough to keep up with the other excellent students. Three students who were at Bronx Science during my time there received the Nobel Prize in Physics.

The after-school clubs were lots of fun, and I especially enjoyed codebreaking. I also joined the bowling club (mainly to be able to hang out with the boys,) the drama club, the astronomy club and several others. Most of the students were younger that their usual grade level indicated because they had skipped grades. Several of the senior boys were only 15 years old and, from my point of view, were not boyfriend material. I considered them as "pear-shaped", but I fell in love with a senior boy who was athletic looking and trim. I will spare him the embarrassment of naming him.

The great thing in school was that most of the students were Jewish and there were no anti-Semitic incidents. Tests were not scheduled on Jewish holidays, and it was taken for granted that the Friday class schedule ended early. This was fortunate as I had to take a long subway ride, from uptown Bronx down to 59th street in Manhattan, and then change to another uptown train to uptown Manhattan. It was a long trip and I was always afraid that I would get home after Shabbat had started.

The trial of Julius and Ethel Rosenberg, accused atomic spies for the Soviet Union, was held while I was at Bronx Science, and all of the students were very caught up in the details. The Rosenbergs were Jewish, and the Jewish community feared the outcome. We were all convinced that the Rosenbergs were innocent of spying, and I attended demonstrations supporting their innocence. After a brief, and in my opinion "unfair" trial, Julius and Ethel Rosenberg were convicted and were executed by electric chair at SingSing on June 19, 1953, while I was a student at City College of New York. I attended an all-night vigil for the Rosenbergs before the death sentence was carried out and was terrified that my parents would find out that I'd attended the vigil. Our Jewish community was traumatized because it wanted to demonstrate that Jews were good loyal citizens.

Finally, An Apartment

My parents finally found a studio apartment during my senior year of high school. As a Jew would say, it was a *Mechaiye,* to live for! We had a door that could be locked, and had our own bathroom. There was a tiny kitchenette and a view of the Hudson River. The apartment was on the 11th floor of a high rise, and the orthodox Jewish tenants on the upper floors had to climb a lot of stairs on Shabbat to avoid using the elevator. There was an elevator man and a doorman, so I felt safe. There was only one room in our studio that was converted from a living room by day to a bedroom by night, by pulling out the couch into a double bed and by setting up a cot for me. My Dad spent alternate nights on duty at the hospital, and when he was home, I slept on the cot. I was always afraid to go to sleep because I feared that my parents might have intimate relations and I wanted to be able to flee quickly. Thankfully, it never happened.

The apartment was on 95th Street and Riverside Drive and was close to Columbia University, located on 116th Street. This gave me an opportunity to attend the Israeli Folk Dance Club at Columbia University that started my lifelong passion for Israeli folk dancing. At the time, I thought nothing of walking alone at night along the Hudson River Park to go to the dance club, and then walking home again at midnight. Today that would be unthinkable. The club went to the pier every time a boat left for Israel (after 1948). We danced on the pier as the ships left, and I became a passionate Zionist during this period.

I had plenty of opportunity to get babysitting jobs in our apartment house, and I also worked at Barton's Kosher candy store on Saturday evenings and Sundays. The owners were observant Orthodox Jews, so the work hours began after Shabbat was over, late in the evening. The store didn't open until 10:30 PM in the winter so we had only one hour of work. I needed to work because I wanted to save money so that I could get my nose "fixed" as the many other Jewish girls did. The "Banana Nose" slur still stung me, and I was determined to get a Hollywood ski-jump nose like Jane Wyman, Ronald Reagan's first wife. When I had accumulated enough money to have the surgery (which my parents would have never allowed) I realized that if I had the "nose job" I wouldn't have enough money for college. I made the better choice to go to college instead of getting nose surgery.

Finally An Apartment

One of the delights of our 11th floor apartment was a spectacular view of the Hudson River. Huge blocks of ice flowed down the river in the winter, and the trees in the spring were unbelievably beautiful. The river was always changing and there were wonderful sunsets. I always enjoyed looking out of our window until one horrible day. As I admired the view, I noticed a woman sitting on a window ledge a few floors above me. At first I thought she was washing her windows, but I soon realized that I was wrong. She wasn't window washing. I ran to warn the doorman but tragically I was too late. The windowsill was deserted. An ambulance arrived shortly afterwards and the result was dreadfully clear.

Another Sexual Attack

My mother was delighted to have an apartment where she could invite guests. She invited friends and family members, and we often had a jolly time eating and *schmoozing*. One of our frequent guests was a man who seemed to be lost and unhappy. My mother explained that the family had been in a death camp and his wife and daughter had not survived. His daughter would have been my age had she lived, and I was told to be especially nice to him because of his loss. I never liked this man and tried to avoid him, but I couldn't. He always managed to leave something at our apartment and would return on another day to retrieve his item, always when my parents were not at home. When I let him in, he tried to sexually assault me, and I bit and kicked him until he gave up. I never told my parents because I was afraid that it would cause a family scandal, and I was afraid that no-one would believe me.

Getting into College

Most of my senior class at Bronx Science went on to The City College of New York, or to one of the other local universities like NYU, Hunter and Queens. I was delighted to be accepted to City College and be among many classmates from Bronx Science. I majored in biology and pre-med, with an interest in going into research. The faculty was marvelous, and my biology professors were very knowledgeable and supportive. The rest of my professors were excellent, and the classes were small. I loved the comparative anatomy class and couldn't get enough of the lab. We dissected dogfish, cats, suckling pigs and other animals and I was astonished to see the commonalities of the various organs in these animals. There was evolution, right there in front of my eyes. On the final practical, there was an exhibit of a very long sharp pointy bone that we were supposed to identify. The clue was to think of the title of a novel. I finally thought of "Oliver's Twist" but the professor had "Moby's Dick" in mind.

The exhibit was the penile bone of a whale. That made me think of "Oliver's Twist." I got credit for the answer.

My favorite animals were bats. Their amazing navigation abilities involving the use of sonar was astonishing. Millions of the blind creatures would emerge from caves and not bump into each other. My professor kept bats, and his enthusiasm for their flight prowess was infectious. I was amazed the huge number of insects the bats devoured. The surprise of seeing the similarities of scales, feathers and hair set me on fire about studying genetics and evolution. It totally disavowed my believing in human "races. "I realized that there was only one race, the Human Race, *Homo sapiens*. All of Hitler's talk of "superior races" was a bunch of bullshit. His Aryan Race concept was utter nonsense. Hitler considered the Jews as belonging to a race, ignoring the fact that people can convert to Judaism. Skin color differences between population groups are based on the amount of melanin, a pigment that protect our skin from UV rays. I could not imagine how the presence of melanin in skin could be linked to intelligence or any other trait. I integrated my love of biology with my sense of social justice and decided that I would dedicate myself to trying to explain that "race" was just a stupid social construct. Sadly, 70 years later, the nonsense of "race" is still influencing our society.

Curriculum at City College

The courses in math, history, German literature, geology and writing were fantastic. I was amazed to discover that there was glacial polish on the rocks in Central Park, the evidence of a previous ice age. Modern German literature was marvelous and I read several books by Thomas Mann, Franz Kafka and others. I was a lousy student in history and government although I enjoyed the classes. I audited music classes and heard fabulous student concerts. My most difficult class was writing, and my professor was very generous with his red pencil. My first paper was red-penciled with many corrections. He was fastidious about grammar and style and was a fabulous teacher but I felt shocked and hurt by his many corrections. I felt better after I found out that the other students had similar comments on their papers. Many of today's journalists and writers would have failed his class. I had to struggle to get a "C" in my writing class. My professor would have murdered anyone who said, or wrote, "I'm like" or "you know" repeatedly in a sentence.

There were "student houses" on campus designed to group undergraduates together for social purposes. City College had over 80,000 students divided between two campuses, with daytime and evening sessions. Many of the students worked during the day and most were from poor, immigrant and work-ing-class families. My belonging to a student house allowed me to make friends and attend social events. My student house had mainly Jewish students who were ardent Zionists, and we had many programs that included Israeli folk dancing, Jewish holi-days, bicycle trips, hikes, singing and partying. The house was a great place to spend gap times between classes, and I could study and get help with homework from the more advanced students. It was a home away from home, and much more pleasant.

My Awkward Date

I met a student at one of the house parties who seemed inter-ested in getting to know me. The object of going to a party was to be taken home afterwards, and that was considered "scoring." The student and I lived far apart, in different boroughs, and we traveled in opposite directions at the end of the evenings. Before we parted for the evening we would make a date to meet at The Museum of Modern Art where there was a series of wonderful movies. Each time we met we made an arrangement to meet again. There were no phone calls because my father didn't allow calls, so no-one was able to leave a name or number. The student had remembered my name from the first time we met, but I didn't remember his, and I was too embarrassed to ask.

This situation went on for over a year and we became very close, without my knowing his name. One day he picked me up at my parents' apartment, and it was my bad luck that my father was at home. How should introduce him to my father? I finally made up a name and introduced him with it. After we left, he asked me why I had used that name. I was embarrassed and had to finally confess that I didn't know his name and we both had a big laugh. His name was Ben.

Greeting my father with a "date" was a big strain. My father treated everyone as a patient, and he would immediately take out his stethoscope, look down his throat, thump his chest, take his pulse and blood pressure and give a first-class physical exam. The poor fellow endured this, but I was both embarrassed and amused. I tried to explain to my father that he should just shake hands and say "hello" but that was impossible for him. He would explain that he was a doctor, after all. He demonstrated this with his peculiar handshake. He would hold the hand of a visitor, extend his middle finger to the wrist, and press on the area where he could feel the pulse of the visitor. It was similar to the 'secret" handshake of the Ku Klux Klan, of which he was not aware.

My Dad's Unhappiness

My Dad still did not have a regular NY State Medical license and that he made him miserable and almost impossible to live with. He took the New York State medical exams three times a year, for 8 years, before he finally passed. We had to stay extremely quiet during those years and make no noise so that he could study. He insisted on no radio, no phone calls nor visitors while he was studying, which was most of the time. His notes and medical books were strewn all over the table and chairs, and we were not allowed to touch or move anything, so we had to sit on the floor. I admired my father's perseverance and determination to continue to take the exams, but he was a tyrant.

The New York medical licensing board exams had a very

low "pass" quota for Jewish immigrant doctors. The AMA of New York was able to identify who was a Jewish immigrant by the name of the applicant. My father's name was Samuel Simche Kalter, definitely a Jewish name, and he finally passed the New York exams in 1954. What ended the New York State Medical Associations' strategy of failing Jewish émigré doctors was the change from having a name to a number on the examination paper. Jewish immigrant doctors had previously been identified by their names, but the numbering system foiled discrimination based on Jewish-sounding names. Suddenly, Jewish immigrant doctors passed their exams.

One of my father's idiosyncrasies was that he would eat only freshly baked rye bread bought at the Tip Toe Inn, located on Broadway and 72nd Street. He would not eat bread from any other bakery. Although he was not an observant Jew, he always fasted on Yom Kippur. We prepared for the Break-the-Fast on the day before Yom Kippur, but he insisted on fresh bread, not be bought the day before. Towards the end of the fast day I was told to walk from 95th on Riverside Drive to 72nd Street on Broadway, to buy bread at the Tip Toe Inn, over 27 blocks away, and I wasn't allowed to take the bus because it was a High Holy Day. On the way home, after walking about 50 blocks, I became faint because of the fasting and from the cold wind from the Hudson River, and I decided to take the bus home. Dad immediately noticed that I arrived home earlier than expected, and he hit me when he found that I had taken a bus on Yom Kippur. I couldn't understand how he could beat me on Yom Kippur (a day of forgiveness). It seemed incomprehensible and I had a hard time forgiving him. I think that he really loved me, but he did not know how to express feelings, except anger.

Summer Jobs

I spent several summers while I was in junior high school as a "mother's helper" a miserable job, but I could live in the mountains or at the beach with the families of the children. I didn't enjoy the babysitting or their parents, but it was wonderful to get out of the stifling hot and humid city. I spent one summer in Long Beach on Long Island and got a beautiful tan to the dismay of my father who was convinced that I would get melanoma. I developed strong and chunky legs from playing beach soccer.

When I was older I worked in one of the kosher hotels in upstate New York during high school and college vacations. My favorite resort hotel was a large and beautiful hotel in the Adirondack Mountains near Lake George. The hotel had hundreds of guests and a huge staff, so I had plenty of social life. My first job was at the Lake George Hotel as an elevator operator. The pay was dismal and, since most of the low pay was deducted for laundry services and for our uniforms and meals, I had to depend on tips to save money for college. I pretended to smile when the guests invariably said, "this job has its ups and downs."

Families usually came to the hotel for a period of two weeks to get away from the heat in New York City. The fathers stayed for weekends and return to the city during the week. I discovered that the way to get tips was to make an arrangement with the mother of the family to warn her if her husband came back early, so that if she had a lover in her bedroom, he could leave in time. I was appalled and shocked at the behavior, but it was lucrative financially but I never "told" on either partner. The fathers would tip me to "keep an eye" on their wives, so I was involved with both sides of their indiscretions. The other way to get tips was to help room service deliver food for some of the families on Jewish fast days. The vacationers did not want to be seen in the hotel dining room on fast days. The guests were very hypocritical, and I felt sick for going along with this scam. After a few weeks, I asked the Maître d' for a waitress job in the dining room. He seemed agreeable but asked if I was "a lying down waitress." It took a while for me to understand what he meant, but I did get a job in the dining room with a station that was far from a window and a long way from the kitchen because

I didn't agree to sleep with him. The cooks also asked the same question and, when I replied with a strong "NO!" I often got bad cuts of meat with lots of fat, or a different vegetable than the one the guest had ordered. All of this went on with a Rabbi in the kitchen to oversee *Kashrut* (Jewish food laws.)

The guests at the Lake George hotel were mainly European Jewish immigrants or their descendants, and they enjoyed living like royalty at the sumptuous Lake George for two weeks before going back to their dreary and underpaid jobs in New York. They put on airs and seemed to enjoy ordering the staff around and making complaints about our service. One couple at my station spoke in German and, referring to me, said something like, "Isn't it a pity that she is a waitress?" They uttered the word "waitress" as though I were a prostitute. After that comment, which they were sure I didn't understand, I went over to them and asked them, in German, what they wanted for dessert. At the next meal, I found that they were sitting at another table. I lost my tip, but I thoroughly enjoyed their embarrassment.

The facilities at the Lake George hotel were wonderful. There were swimming pools, canoeing, rowing, tennis, evening dances, great shows, horseback riding and all sorts of musical entertainment. The staff had a great time using the facilities when guests were not using them. Many of the evening shows had bands that became famous and entertainers who eventually became well known stars. The drawback was that our sleeping facilities were in the wings of the theater and dressing rooms, and the entertainers had to get dressed and stay in our rooms between sets, so we couldn't sleep until the shows were over and they frequently lasted until 5:00 AM.

The Catskills was once the Jewish equivalent of the Riviera. It teemed with bungalow colonies and fancy hotels, luring Jews of all classes with the promise of fresh air and relaxation. Many of immigrant Jews have fond memories of family trips to places with glamorous names like the Nevele and the Concord, the Tamarack Lodge and the Windsor Regency—or to others with more *heimische* names like Grossinger's, Lansman's and

Kutsher's. Legendary comics got their start there: Woody Allen, Milton Berle, Mel Brooks, Lenny Bruce, Sid Caesar, Billy Crystal, Phyllis Diller, Jackie Mason, Carl Reiner, Joan Rivers, and Jerry Stiller. Musical and comedy stars-to-be graced Catskills supper club stages. Sammy Davis, Jr., Benny Goodman, Joel Grey, Madeline Kahn, Barry Manilow, Bette Midler, Barbra Streisand, and Sophie Tucker were regular entertainers. Clean-cut young Jewish men put themselves through college by washing dishes, dancing with *bubbes,* and leading lawn games and conga lines. Even Nobel Prize-winning physicist, Richard Feynman, was once a lowly young waiter there.

Getting into Cornell

My very dearest friend, Rose Goldman, invited me for a weekend at Cornell University where she was studying microbiology. Rose was a brilliant student who was excited about her studies at Cornell. I accepted her invitation and took the bus to Ithaca, NY, to visit her on a football weekend. The campus was gorgeous with beautiful trees in their autumn colors and the creeks were overflowing with rushing water. The scenery was totally different from New York City, and the atmosphere was calm and soothing. The Finger Lakes region of New York was unbelievably beautiful, and I decided to move to Ithaca, if at all possible. I knew that I could never afford to go to Cornell and that was a discouraging thought, but Rose assured me that the microbiology major was in the School of Agriculture, which was part of the U.S. Land Grant System set up by Congress. Land Grant colleges receive government money so there was no tuition for students. Here was the chance I longed for. To leave home, go to a beautiful area and study a major that would prepare me for medical school or graduate school. I didn't dare apply because I had no confidence, but Rose insisted that I try, saying I had nothing to lose. To my amazement, I was accepted for the second semester of the sophomore year. I was delighted to be able to leave home where family life was dominated by my father and his studying.

Life in The Cornell Dorms

I lived in the Freshman dorm because I was a transfer student. I didn't like the arrangement because there were many programs designed solely for freshmen and there were many restrictions. The young women students seemed vapid, privileged, rich and snotty. I had to serve them at the table in a style called "gracious living" which now reminds me of the TV show, Downton Abbey. The place settings had painted porcelain plates with a picture of a peacock, and the waitresses had to set the plates with the peacocks' tails pointed down. Knives, forks and spoons had to be placed in the correct order, with every item facing the proper way. The most annoying custom was that we could not interrupt any conversations at the table in order to ask if the girls wanted seconds, and "coffee, tea or milk." Many of the girls talked endlessly about their dates for the coming weekend and would fail to respond to my menu order requests. Placing a pitcher of water, milk or coffee on the table was not considered gracious. The girls' major objective was getting a "Mrs." in front of their names by their senior year, preferably from a fraternity man or a football player. Their most urgent concern was which cashmere sweater they would wear to the next football game.

Women had to wear skirts in the dining room and this was a big problem during the icy winter months. Waitresses had to wear uniforms with removable buttons, which was very time consuming because the buttons had to be attached to the uniform with clumsy clips. I didn't have time to change from a skirt to pants before my classes after meals, so I devised a method of rolling up my pants' legs and wearing a large skirt over the pants. It was a bulky but effective solution, with the uniform covering everything. We had to work three meals a day, so this transformation became an unending chore. The walk to the Agriculture campus was uphill and long (over a mile), so I was usually late for my classes. Today students today eat "cafeteria-style" and are allowed to wear pants, and waitresses don't have to wear uniforms anymore.

A major activity in the girls' dorms was giving each other Toni Home Permanents. We all cut each-others' hair and then curled it. The rooms smelled of the chemicals that were used for the permanents. This seems ridiculous to me today.

My first roommate, in a women's cottage, was a humanities major who took only three courses a semester. Her class load was light and she had no labs. She was very nice but was a heavy smoker, with lots of reading that she did mostly at night. My schedule was filled with labs and lectures, and I had to squeeze in my waitress job in between the classes. In short, my roommate and I were completely incompatible. I was surprised to get permission to move into the Freshmen dorm with a roommate who was a lot more compatible. A new problem was that I had to get up in the dark—to walk from my dorm to the dorm where I had my waitress station. Daylight appeared at about 8:30 AM but the waitresses had to be in the dining room at 6:00 AM in order to eat and set up breakfast before the women students came. I was able to walk or bicycle to my first class, just as the sunlight started to appear.

Meeting Hugh At Folk Dancing

A wonderful thing happened to me during my first year at Cornell that totally changed my life. I went to the Cornell folk dancing group one evening and saw a young man leaning against the wall with one crutch, one leg in a cast, and the opposite arm in a cast, with a huge gash on his head. I went over to him and asked him why he came to a dance without being able to walk. He looked young and shy and replied that he could only use one crutch because the right arm was broken. I was stunned because I had never seen anyone that bashed up before, certainly not coming to a dance. We chatted briefly and then I went off to dance the evening away. Several months later I met this student again on a hiking club event, and we started to chat. I had been practicing the sport of "gunnelling" on a canoe in the river and he noticed my efforts. Gunnelling involved standing astride the canoe, with feet on the gunnels, while pumping up and down to make the canoe move forward, without falling into the water. I won the race and he came over to me to congratulate me. His arm and leg had healed enough for him to walk, so we went for a stroll. I found out that his name was Hugh and that he had survived a 70 foot free fall from a rock ledge in New Mexico and had been rescued by a local army unit stationed nearby. He had been the lead man of his group of four climbers and had reached the height of 35 feet above his second man. He should have hammered in a piton but he hadn't, and he stepped out on a rotten rock out cropping which gave way. He fell the 35 feet to his second man and then an additional 35 feet below him to land on a rock ledge.

Hugh being rescued after his 75 foot fall onto a ledge
(1953)

Hugh's rescue involved an army unit that took two days

lowering him off the mountain, tied onto a stretcher. He spent three weeks in a hospital with numerous surgeries. He had gangrene in his right arm, which had come apart at the elbow, and there was discussion of having the arm amputated. Fortunately, antibiotics and lots of tissue scraping, saved the elbow and the arm. Hugh entertained me by telling about squeezing out the ants that had crawled into his elbow wound during the long, cold night while he was waiting for his rescue team to return. He told me that as he was lowered in the stretcher from the stone ledge he felt that he was going to slide off and have another big fall. He said that the cold and the thirst had been the worst discomfort of the accident, much more than the pain.

I was completely fascinated by his story. Up until Hugh, the other male students I met were boring, but Hugh was a first-class genius. Hugh told me that he had spent the night on the ledge watching the Perseid meteor shower that bursts into light in August, and I was able to impress him a little with my limited knowledge of astronomy. All this came to nothing between us, as we were both hard-working students and had no free time. A few months later I met Hugh again at folk dancing, and we reestablished our acquaintance. I found out that he was a physics graduate student who lived in the physics building, Rockefeller Hall, or "The Rock" as he called it. He saved money by working in the physics department as one of two live-in fire watchmen crew. Hugh received the free room (a former lab) for staying nights in the building, checking out the fire alarm bell on a weekly basis and being able to climb down a rope from the 3rd floor in case he needed to escape.

Rockefeller Hall

John D. Rockefeller, the philanthropist, had donated a large sum of money to Cornell to build a physics building named after him. His gift required that the building be esthetic and be prepared to house modern physics research. He promised that if the building satisfied his requirements he would give an equal amount of money to furnish the building. Unfortunately, the university misunderstood the terms of the contract and thought that the amount of money initially promised included the expense for installing laboratories with modern instrumentation, so the building was built in the cheapest possible way. For example, the central stairway was built with wood rather than brick, to save the money for furnishing the labs. Rockefeller was so distressed that he refused to give the second portion of the bequest. The central wooden staircase for the four-story physics building did not qualify for fire insurance so in order to qualify for fire insurance so Cornell had to hire two full-time fire wardens. Hugh was lucky to become a fire warden, and he shared a converted physics lab with another graduate student. They paid no rent in the physics building. The roommates became good friends and alternated their on-duty days and nights . Hugh was able to save a great deal of money on housing because of this arrangement. The lab had vacuum lines, gas outlets, counter tops and all of the requirements of a physics lab, so Hugh and his roommate bought cots, a refrigerator, installed a phone and were able to cook and sleep there. The worst part of the job was testing the fire alarm on a weekly basis. The alarm was extremely loud and could wake the dead. There was a thick long rope in the window so that they could make their escape if there really were a fire. We had many parties in the physics building's large lecture halls-all illegal, of course.

Becoming Friends with Hugh

Our "dates" were mainly "study dates." Hugh corrected problem sets for the course for which he was a teaching assistant, while I was studying biochemistry and bacteriology. I was fortunate in having Hugh check my math, physics and chemistry problem sets, and I wound up with a great GPA. We studied a great deal and Hugh was able to manage doing his graduate research and hold a teaching assistantship. Later, he accepted a research assistantship with Professor Hans Bethe, and afterwards worked in the Aeronautical School of Engineering under Dr. Arthur Kantrowitz. These appointments enabled Hugh to go through graduate school in record time.

As time went on I became braver and bolder about inviting a guy on a date, and after a few weeks of our friendship I invited Hugh to a Purim party-the celebration of the Jews having the courage to fight for freedom to worship, freedom of the weak over the strong and from extermination in the ancient Persian Empire. The tradition includes having Purim plays based on the theme of the struggle of the Jews to live in the Persian Empire. I asked Hugh if he would be interested in joining my group's Purim play, and he accepted, not knowing how I would cast him. I cast him in the role of Haman, the villain in the story. Hugh enjoyed being Haman and did a great job. He had a good sense of humor about being the bad guy in a Jewish play. Hugh originally came from rural Arkansas (he was a free range kid in the woods) and had never met a Jew before attending Stanford as an undergraduate. Even there he had encountered very few Jews, so this was new to him and must have seemed very strange.

One of the many things that impressed me was that Hugh subscribed to *I.F. Stone's Weekly* Newsletter, which showed me that he had a strong social conscience. He was also a nature lover who enjoyed camping, hiking and cycling, activities that I enjoyed, and he was very involved with conservation. Hugh seemed generous, caring and was well informed about politics and history. He was certainly not a one dimensional or boring person.

Hugh's Thesis advisor, Professor Philip Morrison

Professor Phil Morrison, Hugh's thesis advisor, was a brilliant physicist and a renaissance man. He contracted polio when he was a youngster and spent many years in bed, reading prodigiously. He was known for his work in quantum physics, nuclear physics and high energy astrophysics. "He had studied at the University of California, Berkeley, under the supervision of J. Robert Oppenheimer, and he also joined the Communist Party at that time." In 1942 he was recruited to work for the Manhattan Project and in 1944 he moved to the Project's Los Alamos Laboratory in New Mexico, where he transported the core of the Trinity test device to the test site, in the back seat of a Dodge sedan. As leader of Project Alberta's pit crew, he helped load the atomic bombs on board the aircraft that participated in the atomic bombing of Hiroshima and Nagasaki. After the war ended, he traveled to Hiroshima as part of the Manhattan Project's mission to assess the damage. Professor Morrison became a champion of nuclear nonproliferation, wrote for the Bulletin of Atomic Scientists, and helped found the Federation of American Scientists and the Institute for Defense and Disarmament Studies. He was also a monthly contributor to the Scientific American magazine writing reviews of science books. He was one of the few ex-communists to remain employed and academically active throughout the 1950s, but his research turned away from nuclear physics towards astrophysics.

Cornell tried to fire Professor Morrison because he was controversial, and because of his former Communist Party affiliation, but he received a great deal of support and remained on the Cornell faculty until he left to go to MIT. Morrison inspired Hugh greatly, and Hugh, too, became active in nuclear nonproliferation during his career. This was ironic, as Hugh spent a major part of his physics career at the Livermore National Radiation Laboratory in California where, as he said, he "bit the hand that fed him."

Microbiology Major

I continued my major in microbiology and biochemistry and loved my classes. Some classes, such as pathogenic bacteriology, were given in the veterinary School, and I enjoyed handling the animals and became very passionate about animals and their well-being. My course in population genetics invited a famous professor of population genetics, Professor Sewall Wright to give a seminar. His expertise was in the inheritance of guinea pig coat colors. He wrote many complex equations on the board to explain the evolution and transmission of the genes for the colors and had several guinea pigs in his lab coat pockets to illustrate the coats. During his lecture and, in a moment of confusion and excitement, he reached for an eraser but grabbed a guinea pig instead, and began to erase the board with the poor pig. The guinea pig squeaked, but Dr. Wright never noticed and the board was wiped clean. We roared with laughter.

Through my connections with Hugh and his major professor, Dr. Philip Morrison, I obtained a job in the biophysics lab that Dr. Morrison established. Biophysics was a completely new field and Morrison, who a visionary, hired Drs. Erwin and Ethel Tessman to establish a lab. I was extremely fortunate to have the job of counting bacterial colonies in the Petri dishes in their lab and getting first hands-on experience with research. Needless to say, I loved it. The lab was located in the new Nuclear Physics lab where Hugh had an office, so we spent a great deal of time together. I was taking a course in bacterial genetics at the time, and one of the scientific papers we were expected to read was the now-famous paper by Watson and Crick on the physical properties of the DNA molecule being the agent of genetic transmission. The close proximity to the Tessmans in Dr. Morrison's lab was instrumental in helping me understand the significance of one of the most famous and fundamental papers in genetics. The thrill and excitement was overwhelming. I was determined to pursue this in my graduate work. I was able to continue in this line of research and spent two years showing that a mathematical model, the Luria-Delbruck Fluctuation Test, was able to explain sexual inheritance in the common intestinal bacterium, *E. coli*.

Another breakthrough through my association with the physics graduate student crowd was to meet a young couple who had just had a baby and were breastfeeding him. I had to do a research paper and chose the subject of the microbiome—(yes, in 1953!) and I isolated *Lactobacillus bifidus* from the diaper contents of their newborn baby. This organism is found only in breast-fed infants during the first few days after birth. My professor was astonished that I accomplished this project since very few students had the luck of knowing a breast-fed baby.

Summer Job in the Catskills

During the summer break of my junior year I accepted a job at a Jewish hotel in the Catskills. It soon became apparent that this was not going to be a good season because there were very few guests. After three weeks, I received a letter from Hugh asking me to visit him at Los Alamos where he had a summer job, and the invitation was very tempting. I obviously was not continuing with my waitress job, clearly a bust. I told my parents that I wanted to quit my job and take a trip to California to visit my Uncle Max Katen and his wife, Rosl, who lived in San Francisco. My parents were delighted in my apparent new interest in family, and happily gave me permission to go. Only then did I mention I might take a side trip to Los Alamos, New Mexico, to visit a "friend." I don't think they understood that the "side trip" was far out of the way from my stated itinerary and that the "friend" was my non-Jewish boyfriend.

Trip to Los Alamos

The plane flight was too expensive, so I decided to go by Greyhound bus on a 5-day trip to the West Coast, with a side trip to

Los Alamos. There was a disaster immediately. By the time we approached Chicago, the Greyhound Company had a drivers' strike on its hands. I was going to be stuck in Chicago until the strike was settled, if ever! Luckily, I found out I could take local buses from city to city and that my Greyhound ticket would be honored. The local buses had no toilet facilities and did not schedule "rest stops" where one could buy food and drink. I travelled like this for three days and nights through the hot midwest summer until I arrived at Denver. There were no commercial buses from Denver to Albuquerque, so I took a local bus for migrant Mexican farm workers in which I spent the night fending off the groping farm workers, trying to keep them from pushing their hands down my blouse. I tried to get the attention of the driver who only laughed at my predicament. I hadn't eaten in three days and was hot, sweaty and scared. I arrived in New Mexico at about 6:30 AM in the morning, and couldn't get off the bus quickly enough. I took a shuttle bus from Albuquerque to Los Alamos and got to the gate only to be told that I could not enter because there was no pass on file for me. The local busses had gotten me to Los Alamos a day earlier than the Greyhound would have, and my pass was for the following day. What to do?

Los Alamos was a "closed city" at that time. Employees needed security classifications because the laboratory was doing nuclear weapons development and building nuclear weapons. The location was the "secret" site of the Manhattan Project, where the US Atomic Bomb was developed in the 1940s—built and tested under the direction of J. Robert Oppenheimer. For this reason, visitors had to have specific invitations and had to be vetted and needed passes to enter. Hugh had arranged for a pass for me, but it was for the following day. I arrived earlier than expected and my pass had not yet been issued, so I could not enter. I asked the gatekeeper to try to contact Hugh's supervisor who rode around on his bicycle to find Hugh. A short time later Hugh arrived and the "pass" issue got settled to my great relief.

Hugh took me to the visitor center, that had a small hotel, and I was able to take a shower and freshen up.

The next two days were exciting. Hugh took me to see Los Alamos and to several amazing archeological sites of the local Native Americans. We climbed into Kivas, explored the countryside and had a great time. In the evening Hugh took me back to the hotel, but I didn't have enough money to stay any more nights. Hugh offered to pay for me, but I was afraid that it would compromise me and that he might want to spend the night with me. These were the 1950s, and "nice" girls wouldn't do a thing like that, so I told Hugh I wanted camp out and that I had a sleeping bag. Hugh told me there were some great camping places that were safe, and he drove me to one of them. He had borrowed a .38 gun from a friend and told me to shoot if anyone bothered me. I was baffled, as I had no idea of how to shoot. I assumed Hugh would camp with me, but that was obviously not what he planned. I had made such a strong case about not spending the night at hotel paid for by him, that it was impossible to ask him to stay with me. I slept in my sleeping bag and swatted mosquitoes all night. I couldn't sleep because the area turned out to be a Lover's Lane area, and cars kept coming to park there. I moved my campsite and the next morning Hugh couldn't find me, but he was relieved to locate me after a bit of searching. He drove me to the bus station and, after we had a breakfast, he told me that he was a confirmed bachelor and wanted to pursue only physics. I took a bus to San Francisco to visit my aunt and uncle and realized that my relationship with Hugh was at an end.

Trip to San Francisco

My uncle and aunt owned a house in the Sunset district of San Francisco, that was large enough to provide me with a guest bedroom that I shared with Uncle Max's shoe samples. Max and Rosl were warm and friendly and full of fun, but they were busy with their jobs and didn't have much time for me, so I spent time by myself just hanging around San Francisco which was a great deal of fun.

My Aunt and Uncle rented a cabin during August near Lake Tahoe and invited me to join them. I had never seen such a beautiful lake before with snowcapped mountains all around. The swimming was wonderful and I enjoyed the beaches and hikes along the shore and even the gambling joints in the Nevada side.

When we returned to San Francisco I was surprised to find a letter from Hugh saying that he was coming to the Bay Area to visit his parents who lived in Palo Alto, and that he wanted to see me. I was delighted to hear from Hugh, and agreed to come to Palo Alto where his parents lived in an old farmhouse surrounded by a six-acre apricot and plum orchard. When Hugh and I arrived, I saw a huge turkey sitting silhouetted against the moon on the old pump house, which was a very strange sight for me. Hugh's mom had lots of chickens, geese, chinchillas, rabbits and other animals, and it was a real treat to visit them. They were very welcoming and treated me hospitably but seemed rather curious about what Hugh and I had in mind.

Trip to Yosemite

Hugh's parents had planned a vacation to camp in Yosemite National Park. We drove together, and I was overwhelmed by the beauty of the Sierra and the dramatic scenery of Yosemite. One morning Hugh and his dad decided to climb Half Dome and invited me to come. We hiked many miles to get to the high country and then to the Dome. It was my first climbing experience, and I was terribly scared but didn't want to admit it, so I went with them. There is a metal cable on Half Dome that made the climbing easy, but on that afternoon we were caught in a sudden thunderstorm. Lightning struck all around. I was terrified the lightning would strike the metal cables. Hugh's dad made a hasty decision to get off the Dome, and we hurried down hoping not to be struck by lightning. Once clear of the dome, we hiked another two hours to the camp. I was scared to death, but felt wonderful in Hugh's company and I realized that I was hooked.

My Stay With Uncle Max and Aunt Rosl in San Francisco

On our return to San Francisco I experienced another dreadful sexual assault. Uncle Max's best friend was a baker who worked all night but was free during the day. One day he arrived at the house while Max and Rosl were at work and tried to sexually attack me. I was terribly shocked and fought him off as hard as I could. I never told Max and Rosl about the attack because I did not want to disturb their strong friendship with the baker, but it scared me terribly and I would never let him in again, even though he returned several times. I was afraid that I wouldn't be believed and accused of fantasizing or exaggerating the incident. I am relieved that the #metoo movement has finally brought attention to this terrible problem. Max and Rosl had plenty of difficulties and didn't need any additional misery. Aunt Rosl's sister had jumped off the Golden Gate Bridge while suffering from depression after immigrating to America and not being able to find a job. This was obviously very painful and I didn't want to add any more to their sorrow.

Uncle Max was a very funny man who always was able to make lemonade out of "lemons." One day, when he was driving to see a client, he received a speeding ticket. He noticed that the policeman was limping and, when he commented on it, the cop explained that his shoes hurt his feet. Uncle Max immediately opened his sample bag and fit the policeman with the most comfortable shoes he had ever worn. As a result the cop took Max to the station and he outfitted all of the policemen with Knapp shoes. They urged him to go to the other police stations and Uncle Max became the shoe supplier of the whole SF police department for many years. Uncle Max boasted that it was the best traffic ticket he ever received.

Back to Cornell, Fall 1954

I took the Greyhound bus back to New York and went back to Cornell for the fall semester and found Hugh waiting for me at my residence. Several of my girlfriends, all very academic types, had been able to find housing in one of Cornell's residential cottages rather than in the big dorms, and we were a very tight and friendly group. All the girls seemed to understand that Hugh and I were now a couple, but I still didn't realize it.

The semester was very busy with school and my dorm waitressing job, and Hugh had a huge load with his physics research and teaching assistantship, so we didn't go out very much, but we were still very close friends. We saw each other but we were pretty preoccupied with academics. I felt that things were cooling off with Hugh, and I applied myself to school and work. The fall semester went by and we were soon at winter break when the dorms were closed.

Sanne and parents, 1954

Engagement to Hugh

The winter break was freezing cold at Cornell with lots of snow and ice. I usually took the bus to go to New York City and visit my parents for a week and see my friends from my high school days. I enjoyed the museums, concerts and plays in the city after living in rural upstate New York, but at the same time, it was always a relief to get back to Cornell and rejoin my group of women friends, now living in a cottage on campus. One evening I planned to wash my hair and go to bed early when the phone rang. It was Hugh. He was on his way home from visiting the Livermore National Laboratory in California where he had been interviewing for a job. Hugh expected to be back in Ithaca within a few hours and wanted to see me. I told him that my hair was wet and, it was freezing outside and I planned on going to bed soon, but he insisted. I couldn't say no. We went out for a walk in the winter night. My damp hair froze solid and I wasn't happy with this outdoor excursion. We soon reached Triphammer Bridge, that spanned one of the many deep gorges on campus. Hugh suddenly stopped in the middle of the bridge and announced he'd been offered a job at Livermore. Not only that, he had received a Fulbright scholarship to Germany and wanted to marry me. I was absolutely flabbergasted. I explained that since I was Jewish, and he wasn't, it was impossible. I certainly would not go to Germany, from which I had escaped many years before. I also told him that my parents would never agree to our marriage, and it was out of the question. He said I should think it over and that we would see each other as much as possible and he would try to persuade me.

Middletown State Mental Hospital

My parents had moved to Middletown, New York, where my father had obtained a position as a psychiatrist in the geriatric section of the State Hospital. He was in charge of 800 elderly patients, many of whom had been institutionalized for years. It was a huge load. Dad had received a Board certification in psychiatry from Columbia University Medical School, and his training in internal medicine, combined with the experience in the Munich Old Age Home, had prepared him well for this position. He received an apartment in one wing of the building where his patients were housed, with only a thin wall between his apartment and the wards. The apartment smelled of urine because many of his patients were incontinent, and shouts and screams were constant background noises. This was the apartment where Hugh visited my parents to tell them that we planned to marry. Hugh went alone because I was too frightened to accompany him because I knew my parents would be opposed to our plans, and I couldn't handle their hysteria.

Hugh took a bus to Middletown and dropped in on my parents without any prior notice. My mother, as usual, was hospitable and invited Hugh for dinner. He ate and ate and ate until my mother had her fill of being a "Jewish Mother." Then he dropped the bombshell that we planned on getting married. Hugh told me that there was a moment of complete silence, and then both of my parents erupted and started to talked simultaneously for about three hours until they both stopped, suddenly exhausted. My father's argument was that Hugh would never advance professionally because he had a Jewish wife. My Mom's argument was that six million Jews had died and I was letting them all down by marrying a non-Jew. Hugh sat through this tirade without saying anything and, by this time, it was too late to get transportation back to Ithaca. My parents invited him to stay overnight, and he stayed for two more days while they talked non-stop, trying to talk him out of marrying me. I didn't hear from Hugh at all during this time (no cell phones in 1955) and I was extremely worried about what might be happening. When Hugh finally returned to Ithaca, he told me my parents were adamantly opposed to our marriage and that they would never attend our wedding, which they didn't.

Conversion (Not)

Hugh decided to convert to Judaism and for us to have a Jewish wedding. We visited the Hillel Rabbi in order that Hugh could start Jewish studies, but the Rabbi turned him down. His comment was "I don't convert people to Judaism for the purpose of the bedroom!" He was very insulting. Hugh approached other Rabbis who also turned him down. We decided that if we couldn't have a Jewish wedding, and that since my parents would never attend our wedding anyway, we might as well just have a civil ceremony. I wanted to wait until Hugh returned from the Fulbright, because I had no wish to go to Germany for a year and re-experience the horrors I had experienced there. We compromised by Hugh's leaving for Germany in September with my joining him midyear, in February, after completing my undergraduate studies at Cornell. My parents were horrified, but we continued to make our plans. I took a heavy load of classes in the fall semester in order to obtain my degree in February, and applied for graduate school at U.C. Berkeley so that Hugh could accept his position at Livermore and I would be in graduate school in the same area.

Hugh's Trip to Germany

Hugh and the other U.S. Fulbright fellows boarded the ship, Italia, in September, 1955, to make the crossing to Germany. Hugh and I continued to make plans by mail while Hugh stayed with a German family, the Brandts, who hosted him on a student exchange program in the tiny town of Rauenberg, near Heidelberg. The German dialect in Rauenberg was so strange that Hugh could not understand a word of what was being said by the Brandt's children. Dr. Brandt and his wife liked Hugh and were very kind to him and immediately helped him with making wedding plans.

Heidelberg Physics Department

Hugh joined the German physics graduate students in Heidelberg University and quickly made friends with his colleagues, but he was disappointed that his major professor, Dr. Hans Jensen, Nobel Laureate in physics, with whom he had planned to do his research, had just left for the USA, on a yearlong professorship. Hugh accepted this news and made the most of things by plunging into learning conversational German, socializing with the other graduate students and the 27 American Fulbright scholars, taking bicycle rides in the wine country and writing long letters to me every day. Of course, he also worked on his physics research. In Heidelberg he lived in a basement room in the home of an elderly couple, the Krabbes, who lived on *Hirschgasse*. The house was near the *Philosophen Weg* within walking distance of the university, across from the Heidelberg Castle ruins by the Neckar River. The district was charming and undamaged from the war, but the Krabbes complained bitterly about the fact that the US army had requisitioned their house after WWII. Hugh had to share a toilet with another student and a bathroom with the Krabbes. He had no kitchen, so he ate at the university mess hall that was subsidized generously. He was able to buy a generous lunch for 40 *pfennigs* and dinner for 80 *pfennigs* (100 *pfennigs* to a Mark, at the time, 10 Marks to 1 USD). Most of Hugh's time was spent working on his research in theoretical physics, so fortunately, he didn't spend much time in his dark basement room.

My Time Back at Cornell, 1955

I spent my last semester busy with courses, studying and writing to Hugh. I planned to take a ship to Germany with a college friend, Lucy Schnayerson, whose husband was stationed in the US Army in Nancy, France. We boarded the ship, the *America*, in February of 1956. Lucy was headed to Le Havre in France, while my original destination, Bremerhaven, in Germany. The crossing was rough, just like my voyage to the US eleven years before, but this was a much larger ship that even had a very fancy dining room. We travelled in tourist class, but it seemed very luxurious compared to the dorms at Cornell. Just before embarking I wrote to Hugh that I would arrive in the port in Le Havre, instead of Bremerhaven, which would cut two days off my voyage. I was impatient to see Hugh again and I didn't want to waste another day at sea. I hoped that he would receive my letter in time to meet me at the correct port. The ship laid anchor at about 3:00 AM, but no one could disembark for several more hours. I was delighted to see Hugh standing on the pier waiting for me. He was half frozen from standing on the freezing pier for half the night.

Europe

Hugh had purchased a little brown Volkswagen that his mom had ordered for herself through Hugh. He could import the little car to the U.S. for her without import taxes if it were used in Europe, so his Mom allowed us to use it as long as we were there. Hugh had driven the VW bug to Le Havre where I was scheduled to arrive. After a few hasty reunion-hugs, we drove the bug to Paris and found a small hotel for a couple of days' stay in Paris.

Paris and Trip across France

Paris was the middle of a freeze and the water pipes at the hotel were frozen. We ate in tiny restaurants and tried to see as much of Paris as possible in two days. I was hobbled by some plantar warts that removed by irradiation from the bottom of my foot. My foot had swollen enormously and I could only get my feet into ski boots. Walking was very painful. None of that mattered as we had a terrific time seeing Paris, seeing men with berets and baguettes and cranky hotel landladies who could not understand our poor French. On the second day, we forgot where we had parked the car, and it took many hours of walking until we found it again. Almost every car in Paris was a little brown Volkswagen, just like ours. We finally found it and we drove across the frozen countryside to Nancy, where my shipmate, Lucy, had an apartment near the US army base. We stayed with friends, Mort and Lucy Rich, for a few days and then headed east towards Germany.

When we left Nancy late in the afternoon, I had the feeling that we were driving in the wrong direction, but Hugh replied we were going the correct way. I was so dazzled by Hugh that I believed everything he did and said. Our destination was Germany and it was late in the afternoon, but we were driving straight into the setting sun. I asked Hugh if Germany was east of France and he replied "yes." Then I asked if the sun set in the west in Europe just like in the US, and he again replied "yes." I waited a few minutes and finally I said that if Germany was east of France and we were driving into the setting sun, it indicated that we were going in the wrong direction. At last Hugh replied "yes" and conceded that we were going in the wrong direction. He tried to regain some dignity by saying that he expected the road would take a sharp turn pretty soon, but he made a U-turn anyhow. This was the first time that I caught Hugh in an error. I was completely disillusioned, and I never let him forget it.

The car's little engine didn't generate enough heat to keep me warm, so I settled down under blankets and eventually fell asleep. I woke suddenly when we stopped by a sign saying "*Zonengrenze*" meaning "border." In front of us was a guard-house with a guard wearing a green uniform who looked exactly like the Nazi guards when I escaped from Germany. In my half-awake state, I believed that I was getting caught leaving Germany and I panicked. The guard looked at our passports and noticed that my birthplace was Munich, so the guard cheer-fully said "*Ach, ein Landtsmann.*" He laughingly waved us through the crossing, but I shook for hours. I was in Germany again.

My Arrival in Heidelberg

We arrived in Heidelberg late at night, quickly found our address, and were welcomed by our landlady, Frau Krabbe, who showed me to the room of student tenant who was on vacation. She explained that I could not stay in Hugh's room because we were not yet married. She could allow me to stay in the other room, while the student was away. The next day, Monday, we went to the City Hall in order to get a marriage license. We were told that we needed an *"Aufenhaldtsehrlaubnis,"* a residence permit, which needed to be signed by our landlord. When we approached Herr Krabbe he obliged and signed, and we went back to the City Hall. Now the German bureaucracy went into full force. The clerk informed us that I needed my *"Geburtzurkunde"* which is equivalent to a birth certificate. Of course, I didn't have this document because I escaped those many years ago without papers. The agent looked at my passport and said, "no problem, just contact the Munich City Hall and they will have the original." I followed his advice and the Munich City Hall sent it by the next mail. This felt really creepy even though it was convenient. First the Germans wanted to kill me, and now they still had my birth certificate on file! Wow! I still existed for the Germans. Hugh and I thought we were ready to get married, but the City Hall did weddings on Tuesdays, Thursdays and Saturdays, with funerals on Mondays, Wednesdays and Fridays. We were going to have to wait until Thursday.

Dr. and Mrs. Brandt Invited Us to Their Home Before the Wedding

We didn't want to stay in our rooms at the Krabbe's house before the wedding. Fortunately we were invited by Hugh's host family, the Brandts, to stay with them for the two days before the ceremony. The Brandts had saved a bottle of wine from their wedding and insisted on toasting us, after which they took us to a restaurant for a very German meal—*Schnitzle* and *Kartoffel*. Beer was the beverage served with dinner followed by a rich dessert with wine. Dr. Brandt insisted that we had to have a brandy before going to bed, and then he and Frau Brandt suggested that Hugh and I share a bedroom. This was unusual for that generation of Germans but we accepted their hospitality and went to bed. Within a few minutes the room started to whirl around and around, and I needed Hugh's help to get to the bathroom. I was drunk and spent the rest of the night in heaving in the bathroom. It was definitely not romantic. Hugh held my head during vomiting fits. Dr. Brandt gave me strict orders to not drink at our wedding and, perhaps, not for the next few weeks.

The Wedding

Now we had the time to organize a wedding party, and we had help from one of Hugh's colleagues, Martin Kretschmar, and his wife, Trautl. We invited all of the physics graduate students and the Fulbright fellows and reserved a restaurant which had been closed for the winter but which opened up just for our party. Hugh's host parents, Dr. and Mrs. Brandt, baked a wedding cake and prepared a bouquet and we were all set for a grand celebration. I still needed to wear ski boots because my feet were still swollen, and I had a black suit and a horribly inappropriate white straw hat, and we were off to get married in a civil ceremony in the Heidelberg City Hall. Somehow it was ghastly but also funny.

A photographer and a reporter showed up at the *Standesamt* (city hall), and were overjoyed to see us. They explained that they were from the U.S. Congressional Fulbright Commission and were doing a story on Fulbright scholars but they couldn't find any in their departments. They checked the physics department, but to their despair, not even Hugh was there. Fortunately one of professors told them that Hugh was getting married that day and they should hurry to the Heidelberg City Hall. They found all of the Fulbright students there, to their great relief. They offered to photograph our wedding. The photographs are now on file in the U.S. Library of Congress.

The lounge at the City Hall was decorated with dreadful pink cupids for weddings and other somber paraphernalia appropriate for funerals. Four other couples were waiting for their turn to get married, and we were all asked which of the prepared wedding speeches the bureaucrat should give. We chose speech #3 without knowing what the text was. I will never forget the contents of speech #3 that was *"Die Ehe ist Eine Sschwere Last"* which translates to "Marriage is a heavy burden". The clerk evidently must have had a very unhappy marriage. He wore what was obviously an old green Nazi uniform, complete with his old shirt that lacked only the Nazi armband. A stripe on the sleeve of his shirt was much darker than the rest of the sleeve, so it was obvious that he had simply torn the Nazi armband off. He asked Hugh if he wanted to marry me, and Hugh stood there, scratched his head, and took a long pause. I thought that Hugh had not understood the German, but Hugh was just teasing me and he finally said *"Ya."* The clerk asked me if I were going to bring up my children as good Germans and I said *"Nein!"* I was afraid that he was going to abort the ceremony, but he was so shocked that he said nothing.

After the ceremony we all went out for coffee and cake and, later in the day, we went to the restaurant on top of the Heidelberg hills, the *Wolfsbrunnen*, where we had our wedding dinner. The chef had shot a deer that day which he prepared for a venison dinner. It was all very festive, and we danced until late into the night. The cost for the banquet was only $50 dollars, and we could hardly believe it. The guests all brought presents. The Brandts' present was a free baby delivery when our first child was born—a novel present. It was so late into the night that there was no public transportation. The German students all walked back to town, but the American students wanted rides. Hugh spent most of the night, after dropping me off, taking many trips in our little brown bug, shuttling the Fulbright students back to town. He finally arrived back at our place at dawn.

Honeymoon

I needed to get my name changed in my passport from Kalter to DeWitt, but in order to do so I had to mail the passport to the embassy in Stuttgart. I was afraid that we would not get it back in time for our planned trip, so we left on our wedding trip with my old passport and old name. When we got to our first stop we were unable to rent a room at a hotel because we had different names, DeWitt and Kalter, and the hotel clerk didn't believe that we were married. It seemed that only the Germans were strict. The hoteliers in France and Austria, our skiing destination, didn't care about the discrepancies in names at all.

Skiing in Austria

We were met in the skiing resort by good old friends from Los Alamos, physicist Dr. Ken Ford and his wife, Karin, who had decided to join us on our honeymoon. (In 2015, Ken published a book on the bomb, "Building the H Bomb: A Personal History.") They were great companions on our skiing adventure, and we danced every evening. The little village of Oberstdorff was located high in the Austrian Alps with snow-white mountains, quaint cuckoo clock stores and beer halls. The ski lessons were inexpensive, and we spent two weeks going up by rope tow and skiing down, mainly on our bottoms. I was a lousy skier but Hugh did quite well. The evenings were spent eating at inexpensive restaurants and dancing Austrian folk dancing to accordion music.

Italy Trip

Hugh and I reluctantly left Oberstdorff and drove over the mountain pass in the Apennines to Italy. I was amazed that people working in the fields waved to us and were extremely friendly. There few tourists in Italy in 1956, and we received very warm welcomes. We visited many cities and beautiful countryside and slept in youth hostels converted from chicken coops, or old US bases, signs still pointing to the commissary and staff offices.

We visited Venice, Florence, Siena, Turin, Palermo, Bologna, Rome, Naples, Padua and Pisa. Many churches, many museums and even a Synagogue in Florence, where the *Gabai* welcomed Hugh, even though he "didn't look Jewish." We had a good laugh about this remark, but it was impossible to explain to the *Gabai*, as we did not know Italian.

The youth hostels were inexpensive and ranged from extremely primitive chicken coops to elegant mansions. The drawback was that women and men had to be accommodated separately—not fun for a honeymoon—and that they were restricted to hikers. We would hide our car about a half-mile from the hostel and then come hiking in with our backpacks.

The hostels were full of young people from many countries who were eager to share what they had seen, and tell how to avoid the tourist traps. One tourist trap that we were not informed about was Capri. Capri is an island located in the Tyrrhenian Sea off the Sorrentine Peninsula, on the south side of the Gulf of Naples. The night before, we had stayed in a youth hostel that was converted from a former US military occupation base. Unfortunately, there were no other young tourists there, so we were un-informed. We bought the cheapest tickets for the boat trip to the Island and congratulated ourselves on the great price. After a lovely two-day stay filled with swimming and hiking, we tried to find a boat to take us back to the mainland. To our shock we had bought a one-way ticket, and we discovered that the return trip cost four-times the amount of the trip to the Island. We had a choice of paying up or swimming back to shore. We had fallen into a tourist trap!

The first Italian city we visited was Venice. As we strolled across the square, Hugh heard a peculiar laugh. There was only one person in the world with a hyena laugh, his professor, Hans Bethe, from Cornell. Hugh had helped Professor Bethe edit a book while he was at Cornell. Sure enough, we spotted the Bethe's across the square, and we had a wonderful reunion.

We ate great food, drank cheap wine and ate terrific Italian ice cream and were always treated in a warm and friendly way. Our stays in bed-and-breakfast places were great, even when we had to sleep in the family's living room. We managed to attended operas, concerts and plays, which we didn't understand, parades and folk festivals. All around us was evidence of the bombings of WWII, although most of the rubble had been removed. There were broken bridges and other damaged structures. WWII was still a visible presence.

The high points of the Italy trip were seeing Michelangelo's statue of David, the Vatican, and the wonderful museums and churches. The Vatican was high on our list, and we were amazed at the contrast between the kitsch in the courtyard and the magnificence of the paintings inside the Vatican. We didn't buy any fragments of Saints' bones" or "Pieces of the Cross," but we bought lots of postcards and took many photos. It was overwhelming. It was easy to understand how Christians could be spiritually moved by the architecture and the art.

The most striking church was completely decorated with

bones; on ceilings, walls and other structures in the church. Vertebrae, rib bones, thigh bones and skulls were arranged in rosettes and other artistic patterns. The bones were the remains of the monks who had worshipped there over the centuries.

We headed back to Germany on our last tank of gas and with virtually no money. Fortunately, the last few miles were downhill, and we were able to roll home. The 1955 model of VW did not have a gas gauge, but it had an idiot stick that we could turn to access the emergency tank. We had to walk the last half-mile to our home.

Life In Heidelberg in Spring, 1956

We settled into a routine, with Hugh going to the physics institute and my taking classes in genetics and biology. I was curious to see how the Germans revived genetics after their Nazi-era propaganda regarding the "Superior Teutonic Race"—the equivalent of the current "White Supremacy" movement. The Nazi era had purged the universities of Jewish scientists and students, so there were many years missing from their academies. I was happy and surprised that the genetics courses were up-to-date, but many of the scientific papers written by Jews were still missing from the biology library.

When I wasn't at classes I wandered through the town and sometimes went to the *Kino* (movies.) This was always amusing because the films that were shown were mostly American Westerns dubbed into German. I found it hilarious that American Indians were speaking German. Just imagine "Hi Ho Silver" spoken in German! One film "*Fawler Pelz*" meaning "lazy fur," was a scary Hitchcock film. I was so frightened I grabbed the guy next to me and hung on tightly. He was extremely accepting and endured my clinging without a word. It was most embarrassing. I apologized, and he simply smiled and said it was "okay." When I wasn't in class or at the movies I gave English lessons to students who wanted to come to the States to study. This was fun, and I also improved my German at the same time.

We made good friends with the physics students and had a lively social life. There were many coffee hours and dinners where we spoke about politics and the horrors of the Nazi era. These were difficult subjects, but the students were very modern and were horrified by Germany's recent history. We took a trip to Munich with one of the couples and visited Dachau, a concentration camp. We saw the sign *"Brause Bahd"* which means "showers" and we felt sick. My family and I had been incarcerated in Dachau in 1938, while it was still a work camp, not yet a death camp, and our German student companions were horrified. We also met some Germans who were still indoctrinated with Nazi ideology and who tried to justify some of the events perpetrated by the Germans. It took a lot of restraint to not argue with them. It would have been hopeless.

We were invited to the apartment of an elderly couple, whom we suspected had been at least moderate supporters of the Nazis. We were asked to bring our USA slide collection, and we obliged with lots of photos of our beautiful National Parks, including pictures of bears, elk, moose and other wild creatures. The old couple had only the vaguest idea of what the USA looked like, that was based solely on Hollywood films. Our slide projector's legs got stuck, and we couldn't crank them up, so Hugh suggested they get a book to brace up the projector. They were happy to oblige with their copy of Hitler's *Mein Kampf*. I was really shocked to see the ghastly book, but I restrained from commenting. Then an odd thing happened! As soon as we propped up the projector on the book, the bulb burned out. It was only a coincidence, but I had a gut feeling that the projector itself decided that this was too much. An annotated edition of *Mein Kampf* was recently published in German in 2016 and has generated lots of interest and controversy.

I enjoyed riding on busses and trains and overheard the German passengers discuss Hugh and me—obvious Americans

—in German. Most of the passengers assumed we couldn't understand German, so we overheard outrageous comments about ourselves. Most of the comments were unpleasant, about how uncivilized and uncultivated Americans were. It was hard to keep from laughing.

From Yugoslavia to Berkeley

We left Heidelberg in the middle of July, during the summer break, squeezed into our little VW, which we had named Pepperl. Our good friends were with us—Martin and Trautl Kretzschmar, and Marika Varga, a young Yugoslavian student who was studying in Heidelberg. We headed south *via* Munich to Austria in our heavily loaded bug. Pepperl was bursting with five people plus camping gear for six weeks. During our stay in Austria, Pepperl developed engine trouble, and Marika's Austrian permit was good for only three days. This was a stressful event, for if she overstayed her visa deadline, she would not be able to re-enter Germany through Austria to continue her studies. The repair shop in Vienna needed to order a part, which delayed us for two days. We had only a few hours before Marika's visa was to expire. We drove off immediately after Pepperl was repaired to cross the Yugoslavian border.

Yugoslavia

Marika was crying with anxiety and was desperately afraid that her permit would expire, so we left late in the afternoon for the

Loibl Pass, an unbelievably steep and narrow road that Pepperl couldn't manage. All of us, except for Hugh, got out of Pepperl, and we hiked up the pass while Hugh drove to the top. We reached the border just before midnight, minutes before Marika's visa expired. The border guards were fast asleep and snoring when we arrived and were astonished to see tourists, especially Americans. They started to inspect our luggage and finally gave up after a few hours of searching, as they were drunk and sleepy. This was a huge relief because we were smuggling kummel (caraway) seeds rolled up in our sleeping bags for Marika's father, who planned to make a liqueur from his kummel crop. Kummel seeds have a very strong odor, so they are difficult to smuggle, but the guards were too drunk to smell our illegal items. The border guards asked Hugh to come inside the guardhouse for immigration formalities, because they had never seen an American before. They finally passed Hugh through the gate and fell back to sleep.

We drove through the Yugoslavian countryside hoping to find a camping place where we could pitch our tents and get some rest. In the morning we found that we were surrounded by a crowd of Roma (Gypsies) who couldn't figure out what kind of people we were. We had a German license plate with an "A" sticker (for Austria) and they tried to figure out if we were Australians, Austrians or Americans. One of the men spoke some German and bargained with Hugh to sell me to him for two cartons of cigarettes and a couple of goats. I was afraid Hugh might accept the offer! When we drove off, the group ran after us shouting "STOP!" To our astonishment, they gave us back the items that they had "stolen" from us, including our cameras and hiking boots. They laughed at being able to pinch our items without our noticing. It was all very good natured.

We continued on to Lubliana, Zagreb and Osijek and drove through beautiful small towns with potted carnations in the cottage windowsills. People in the streets or in their front yards wore their very best clothes, as it was a Sunday, and they enjoyed being photographed by us, especially the lovely young women who had elaborate braided hairstyles. We were shocked at the sight of the older women, who were all in black and had black headscarves. Although they looked old, they were probably only middle aged. They walked with their pigs, all of which wore pink collars. It was a charming and funny sight.

We took Marika to her parents' home in Lug, a small southern Hungarian village a few kilometers from Osijek, on the other side of the river Drava. Marika's father was a former pastor of the reformed-Protestant community of Lug before Yugoslavia became a Communist state. He was not allowed to minister to his congregation during Tito's regime, but he held secret services in their barn. The family prepared and served enormous amounts of food for us and entertained us with folk songs and stories. We had Hungarian paprikash, which was burning hot, and Hugh choked and it almost burned up his insides. We were treated like royal guests, and Marika's father was delighted to receive the kummel seeds, that he was going to plant to make liqueur from his crop. He was restricted to planting crops that the Communists assigned to him, and that did not include kummel.

We continued our journey to Belgrade *via* Uncover and Novo Sad, a distance of several hundred miles. Pepperl did not have a gas gauge, so we had to kick the lever on the emergency tank when Pepperl was out of gas in the main tank. We had only a gallon in the reserve tank to reach the next gas station.

Yugoslavia did not have many gas stations and the tank was completely empty when we finally rolled into a primitive gas station on the highway. The man who was in charge was smoking a cigarette and, as there was no pump, he simply poured gas into our tank from a can while he smoked. I ran as quickly as I could to get far away from the anticipated explosion but fortunately nothing happened. We arrived in Belgrade and were able to stay at a Belgrade University student dorm, as this was during the summer vacation.

By this time Hugh had serious cramps and diarrhea from the paprikash and the broiling heat, and he spent most of the night in the dormitory bathroom. The dorm manager called an ambulance (it was really just a truck with a red cross painted on it) and drove him to the student infirmary. Nurses hurried us past the long line of students who were waiting for their pre-registration medical exams and rushed Hugh to a doctor. The Communists were obviously showing off their free medical services. The doctor prescribed tea, castor oil and rest. The treatment seemed simple, but did the trick. Hugh didn't eat for a couple of days until he was well again. While Hugh was resting, workers came into our room at 5 o'clock in the morning to do some repair work. They told us "don't bother, you can go on sleeping while we work."

Belgrade is one of the oldest cities in Europe, located on the confluence of the Sava and Danube Rivers in Serbia, near the Balkan border. It is huge but is still a great "walking city" with loads of old architecture, museums, churches and fortresses. In the evenings, people had to gather in the great squares for oblig-atory "spontaneous" demonstrations in praise of Tito and Communism. The speeches were endless and probably boring (we couldn't understand them), and the crowd applauded frequently although everyone looked bored.

We drove south from Yugoslavia to Macedonia and Greece over rugged territory. The country was still battered by WWII bombings, and many bridges and roads were not yet repaired, so we were forced to drive through dry riverbeds. We encoun-tered some very threatening soldiers while we were taking a photo of a broken bridge. They tried to take away our cameras to prevent us from taking photos, so we put them into our ruck-sacks and left. We didn't want to get arrested in a Communist State.

Greece

We continued to Greece and arrived late in the evening in Thessaloniki. Locating the youth hostel on our map was impossible, as we couldn't read the Greek street signs. Eventually we asked a policeman who helpfully got into our car and led us to what he thought we were looking for. It turned out to be the city dump. We never knew if he was confused or if he was doing a "payback" because we had a German car with German license plates and was angry about the occupation during WWII. Fortunately, we found a beautiful beach ourselves and decided to sleep on the sand.

In the morning we discovered that we were on a private beach. To our surprise and relief, the owner graciously invited us for breakfast. He had a lovely German wife who couldn't speak Greek and he couldn't speak German. They were obviously very much in love but could speak to each other only in broken English. They invited us to continue camping on the beach and eat and shower in their home. They were wonderful people, genuinely friendly and hospitable, so we were reluctant to leave and continue south to Athens. From Thessaloniki, we drove to Larissa where we had an unforgettably delicious meal of goat meat roasted on a spit, and then we continued on to Lamia and Athens.

We found an inexpensive hotel near the Acropolis and wanted to take showers but, because the weather was extremely hot, and there was a drought, so no water was available for showers. We drank beer and wine to hydrate ourselves and to cheer us up and then drove to the Acropolis, which was more spectacular and awesome than we had ever imagined. We returned often to view it several times. We also visited the museums and other ancient ruins and temples, and we enjoyed the markets and the hustle-bustle of the streets.

Athens

After three days in Athens we drove to the Peloponnesian peninsula *via* Korinth to Epidaurus, where we admired the big ancient theater and explored archeological sites—the most memorable of which was Agamemnon's tomb, nearly 3,500 years old. I wished that I had read the *Iliad* recently. It was deliciously cool in the huge tomb, and we stayed there until evening to escape the heat of the day, because our friend, Trautl, had heat stroke. We slept on beaches and ate tasty food from street vendors. We drove to Olympia, Tyrin, Mykene and Nauplin and explored the archeological sites. Our drive along the Mediterranean seacoast took us past beautiful olive and cypress groves, and we passed fields with sheep and goats guarded by little boys. We attempted to remember the descriptions of the ancient Mycenaean civilizations from Homer's epic stories in the *Iliad* and *Odyssey*. Echoes of Homer were everywhere.

Delphi

We consulted the Oracle in Delphi about our future, but we did not get a response. Instead, a dog came out of the site and bit Hugh on the hand, but not badly. The dog had some puppies and we fed her leftovers from our picnic, so the mother became quite friendly.

Time pressures caused us to start our return north to Germany. We passed through Macedonia again, just to the east of the Albanian border. We were invited by some very friendly Muslim men into their Mosque in a little village. They were very proud of it, because it was decorated with pictures, contrary to Muslim tradition.

Our drive along the shore of Lake Ohrid had spectacular and almost unreal sights. From there we snaked down the high mountains to the Adriatic Sea, ending at the Bay of Kotor.

The Adriatic Coast

The drive north took us through Yugoslavia again, but this time we took the spectacular coastal route. The roads were terrible, and we soon discovered why. There were groups of repairmen who stood around and chatted and occasionally drank some Slivovitz, a strong plum brandy. Their pay was so paltry that they didn't bother to work. This attitude was prevalent everywhere we went, especially restaurants, where the waiters couldn't be bothered to take an order. When they finally asked us what we wanted, they simply disappeared into the kitchen not to be seen again for a very long time, and then they brought something entirely different from what we had ordered. There was no motivation under communism. We ate what we were brought, it was always good.

The coast was stunningly beautiful, and we enjoyed the picturesque towns and beaches. We followed the coast, with stopovers in Dubrovnik, Split, Rijeka and Trieste. The city of Split was lovely, and we stayed there an extra day and then drove northwards *via* Trieste back to Germany. We immediately felt the contrast between the communist countries and the free world where efficiency and promptness were expected.

Back in Germany

We spent the next few weeks in Heidelberg where Hugh worked on finishing his thesis while I tutored English and spent time at the library trying to keep up with genetics journals. We spent some time with the other Fulbright fellows and dined with the many friends we had made. Hugh finally met Professor Jenson who had just returned from his sabbatical in the USA. I don't think Dr. Jenson ever looked at Hugh's thesis or tried to make suggestions or corrections.

The Spring break at the university gave us the opportunity to go on a mountain climbing trip to Piz Palu located in the Bernina mountain range in the Swiss Alps. Piz Palu is about 3905 meters high (about 13,000 feet). with three summits covered with glaciers. We hiked up the mountain to the Diavolezza hut, at the altitude 2973 meters, carrying our crampons and ice axes. After s short night's sleep (up at about 2 AM) we set out to reach the over the glaciers to reach the ridge. We made an early start in order to avoid the avalanches that were a danger in the warm afternoon. Jumping across crevasses and hoping to land on firm ice, rather than the crevice, terrified me. The crest was covered with a cornice of snow and the very next day a group of climbers, all roped together and standing in one place for a photograph, fell to their death when their combined weight broke the cornice which collapsed. We climbed down to the mountain all filthy and sweaty, and we went to a hotel in Zermatt and took baths. It was a great but scary trip.

We left Heidelberg late in September of 1956 and drove to Denmark—our destination, Copenhagen. This youth hostel was a boat moored in the harbor that was ideally situated for sight-seeing. One evening we went to the famous Tivoli Garden where we had fun visiting all of the booths, but when we returned to our car we discovered that it had been broken into and Hugh's briefcase, containing his thesis and our return boat tickets, had been stolen. Fortunately, Hugh had made a copy of his thesis and had mailed it to Professor Morrison at Cornell, but our boat tickets were gone. We aborted our sightseeing in Denmark and drove to Amsterdam, which was the port from which we were booked to return. We hastened to the US embassy and the Holland-America Line ship company to see if they would replace the tickets. We were lucky that they expedited our request, and we were issued new tickets immediately. I was sweaty with worry, but after a few frantic hours, it ended well.

We planned to sail on a Dutch ship to England and spend a few days there before continuing home to New York. One of the first things we did when we arrived in England was to visit Catherine Lukas, who had sponsored my parents' entry to England and saved our lives. She was astonished to see us and was amazed that I was grown up and married. I told her that she had saved our family's life, and my story of my parent's success in the US brought tears to her eyes. I will never forget this generous Christian woman who was willing to risk sponsoring an unknown Jewish family and save us from the Holocaust.

England and Wales

We had no transportation in England as our car was on the ship, so we hitchhiked to Wales to visit another important family in my history. We arrived unannounced at the home of the mine manager's home, and I was reunited with my old school friend, Anne Davis-Jones. Anne, who was to be married that weekend, invited us to her wedding, and we got to see many of my wartime acquaintances. The whole town was excited by our visit, and my elementary school held an assembly where Hugh and I heard the students sing Welsh songs. We were welcomed very graciously and had a chance to meet the new principal and staff. Anne's wedding was beautiful, and we met many of the fellow students from the Llechyvidach School, that I had attended. It was a wonderful reunion—totally unexpected. We also visited Minister Williams and his family who had been very welcoming to my family during the war years.

Back to the USA

We hitchhiked back to Liverpool and sailed to the USA on the Dutch ship, the *Ryndam*, in October of 1956. I was seasick and miserable the whole way, as usual. The Israeli 1956 Suez Crisis (The Franco-British-Israeli War) occurred during our crossing and was over during our Atlantic crossing. We never even heard any news of the news of the October war, which was an invasion of Egypt in response to the Suez Canal nationalization. We had completely missed this world-shaking event.

On our arrival in New York, we went to retrieve our luggage and our car and were horrified to see our little VW bug with its top all bashed in – a squashed bug! The car had been squeezed into the cargo area into a space too small for it, with cars piled above and below, but we were happy to have it back, even bashed in. We drove around New York and collected many parking tickets, but we got away with it since we had German license plates and couldn't be located. We spent a week at my parents' home at the Middletown State Hospital, and my parents were very welcoming and seemed to have forgiven my marrying Hugh. They fell in love with him and treated him like royalty and were eager to hear all about our adventures. They never made any more negative comments since we married.

Mom and Dad in Middletown, 1965

Cornell

We drove back to Cornell where Hugh met with his thesis committee and took his final exam for his Ph.D. There were some revisions to be made in his thesis, which he estimated would take two months to complete so we rented a room from a horrible landlady, Mrs. Keene, who made it a habit to come into our room without knocking. She usually came in the morning when we were still in bed and stood there talking forever. Mrs. Keene had a key to our room, so there was nothing that we could do to stop her. Poor lonely woman!

I was lucky to get a job in the bacteriology department as a lab assistant to Professor John Bonner, an expert in in photosynthesis and plant genetics, and I learned a lot about plant biochemistry and also earned some income. My job helped with the rent for those two months. Hugh taught me how to do calculations on his ancient desktop HP Friden calculator, where I spent many hours calculating data points for his thesis. We were able to renew friendships with Hugh's former colleagues and the time passed very nicely. Hugh finished typing his thesis on his ancient Smith-Corona mechanical typewriter, prepared for his thesis defense (he passed), and then we were finally off to Berkeley, where I planned to go to graduate school, and where Hugh had a job waiting for him at the Lawrence Livermore National Laboratory (LLNL).

Drive to California via Chicago and Arkansas

We set off in Pepperl and drove to Chicago to visit my Uncle Ernst and Aunt Marlise and their two-year-old daughter, Beatrice, and had a lovely time with them. After our visit we drove south to Arkansas to visit Hugh's grandmother on her farm near the Mississippi border. I met Hugh's many relatives, which was a big culture shock for me. Southern hospitality was wonderful, but I was astonished that Hugh's relatives had never met a Jew before. The South was still segregated in 1957—the time of the Little Rock School integration crisis—and the political atmosphere was very tense. Arkansas law defined Jews as a "Race" and had a law against interracial marriages, so Hugh and I were considered an illegally mixed-race couple. Except for that, we had a wonderful visit. We tried to avoid discussing politics, which was fairly easy because everyone wanted only to hear about our adventures.

On to California, February, 1957

We continued on our trip, driving through Texas in a terrifying ice storm. After sliding off the road several times we finally gave up and decided to stay at a motel, which turned out to be fully occupied, but the kind owner allowed us to sleep on a couch in the office. The weather was better the next day, and we were able to continue on to sunny and warm Los Angeles and then north along the Pacific coast to Palo Alto. We had a brief stay with Hugh's parents in Palo Alto to debrief, and then drove to Berkeley, which has been our home ever since. We enjoyed Hugh's parents' warm hospitality, their beautiful apricot and walnut orchards, ducks, turkeys and chickens on their property. Their home was four miles outside of Palo Alto but now the area is called Los Altos Hills. Sadly, all of the apricot and plum orchards have been replaced with housing tracts. Hugh's parents hoped that we would stay in Palo Alto, where they had built a small house for us to stay in, and I could go to Stanford, where I was also accepted, and Hugh could drive to Livermore—about equidistant from the Berkeley drive, but I felt we should live a bit further away from them. We dashed off to Berkeley in order to find a place to live before my registration as a graduate student for the spring semester at UC Berkeley Microbiology Department.

Arrival in Berkeley

The University had a housing rental list, and we quickly signed a lease for a one-bedroom cottage a few blocks south of the UC campus on the corner of Channing and Ellsworth streets. The rent was $85 per month. We settled in and made it our home for about two years. The cottage was located in back of a dentist's parking lot, and on the weekends, we had the whole parking lot to ourselves. We had BBQ's and Israeli dance parties with plenty of space for dancing. Our cottage had a "Dutch Door" with the upper and lower part of the door opening separately. A stray kitten adopted us, and he was able jump in and out of the unlocked upper door while we were away. This seems unbelievable today when there is so much crime in south Berkeley. There was no crime and very little traffic then—an ideal location, just three blocks from campus, where I could ride my bicycle to the Life Science building.

My Graduate Student Time

I was welcomed into the microbiology department by Professor Edward Adelberg who received me wonderfully. The faculty included Professors Roger Stanier and Michael Doudoroff, giants in their fields, who immediately insisted that we were to be on a first name basis. The professors, post-doctoral fellows and graduate students formed a friendly and supportive group, and I was treated warmly and respectfully. All graduate students had to participate in teaching assistantships and research grants and were invited to all of the department's seminars where we met most of the major researchers in the new field of microbial genetics. It was a heady time, and we were welcomed at international meetings and treated professionally. The courses were demanding but interesting, and I was kept very busy for the next few years.

Hugh and I made many friends and we took advantage of the lectures, cultural events, concerts and Israeli folk dancing on campus. We camped, hiked and climbed on our many trips to state and national parks, especially Yosemite. Those were wonderful times.

My research took me into the area of sexuality in bacteria

and the genetics of anti-biotic resistance and dependence. The gene for male sexuality in *E. coli* could integrate into its circular chromosome, which resulted in "Super" or High Frequency (HFr) males and was linked to several genes for antibiotic resistance. Most people were unaware that bacteria (*E. coli*) had sexes, actually three sexes. No-one in the lay public, and not even physicians took notice of the work on drug resistance and independence to streptomycin and penicillin, which Dr. Adelberg and I published. I worked on antibiotic resistance in 1960, but the principles of drug resistance are only now becoming timely and of great concern, because so many bacterial pathogens are resistant to multiple antibiotics.

Bacteria grow rapidly, especially my research organism, *E. Coli*, which replicates every 20 minutes, so I had to return to the lab evenings and weekends to feed and take care of the cells and harvest their viruses. The short trip from our little cottage to the lab made it possible to cycle back and forth to the lab quickly, so Hugh and I had time to be together and enjoy Berkeley in its pre-political days. I frequently returned to the lab after dinner in the evenings, but it was scary being in the huge Life Sciences building at night. Once, when I had to use the ladies' room, I saw a man's shoes in the stall next to mine. I hoped nothing would happen while I was there alone.

The graduate students in the microbiology department got along very well, and we were a close community. The atmosphere was warm and supportive, and Hugh and I often socialized with my fellow students. We did not see Hugh's colleagues often, as most of them lived in Livermore, an hour's drive from Berkeley. We were all teaching assistants (TAs) in the labs where I learned most of my microbiology by teaching undergraduate students. I had great fun correcting the answers on final exams, because the students were very creative in making up answers for questions for which they were not sure of the answers. One "answer" on the definition of venereal diseases: "A venerable disease of the Gentiles." I gave the student full credit, because he might not have known how to spell "venereal" or "genitalia."

There was a tragic incident during my time in the microbiology department. I made close friends with a fellow graduate student, Maria Bernardini, the daughter of an Italian physicist, who was married to a Ceylonese graduate student in the plant pathology department. Maria and her husband were expecting a baby, and Maria's mother came to help during the first few weeks after the birth. There was a huge cultural conflict in their home and one evening Maria's husband called and asked to come over to see us. Unfortunately, we had a prior commitment and I suggested that he come another time. The next morning, I was horrified to find out that he had committed suicide. I regret having turned him down and I wonder if things had turned out differently had we canceled our appointment and allowed him visit. It still haunts me.

Early Berkeley Days

Our little cottage on Ellsworth Street was only three blocks from Telegraph Avenue, now famous for being central to the Free Speech and anti-War movements. In 1957, Telegraph Avenue was quiet, tranquil lined with little shops. There was an elegant furniture store, Frazers, a men's wear store, The Baby Nook, a classical records store called "Record City," Larry Blake's Beer and Food Pub, The Blue and Gold grocery store, and the Cinema Guild and Studio, a theater owned by Ed Landberg and famous film critic, Pauline Kael, which showed classic and foreign films. We were lucky to live in a culturally and intellectually vigorous milieu before it all got spoiled in the '60s. The documentary short "Ed & Pauline" (2014) is all about the famous Cinema Guild.

My Mother's Brother in SF, Max Katen and his Wife Rosl

My uncle Max, who lived in San Francisco in the Sunset District with his wife, Rosl, invited us to dinner frequently. I was a flower girl at their wedding in Munich in 1937, and they were delighted to have Hugh and me come and have dinner with them. They were a wonderful and friendly couple and were extremely hospitable. Uncle Max was still selling shoes for Knapp Company and Aunt Rose was an accountant. They "adopted" us and felt fortunate to have some family from the "old" country.

I loved Max and Aunt Rosl. Tragically Max passed away in 1961 of heart disease. He had contracted Scarlet Fever (Rheumatic Fever) when he was very young, that had damaged his heart. He was a loving and generous man, and he left his wife bereft. She died shortly afterwards of breast cancer.

Hugh Shows Me California

Hugh was very happy to be in California, and during our early years in Berkeley, and he planned many camping trips. My first camping trip was to the Pinnacles National Park, home to cliffs, crags, and cave formations and lots of wildlife such as peregrine falcons, golden eagles, California condors, snakes and raccoons. The raccoons outsmarted us and broke into two gangs; one to distract us, and the other to steal our food. The raccoons had a great time laughing at us. We climbed on the rocky pinnacles, which scared me a great deal.

Our next trip was a mountain climbing trip to Picacho del Diablo in the Baja Peninsula We climbed with good friends from the Stanford Alpine Club (SAC). Picacho del Diablo is 10,157 feet high and is the highest peak in the Baja Peninsula. We had to carry in our food as well as our drinking water, because there are many bighorn sheep and lots of other wildlife that contaminate the streams. All that water made our packs heavy. Our trip leader inspected our backpacks before we started the climb so he could eliminate "unnecessary" items. He came across a package of tampons in my pack and asked, "what are these?" I was surprise at this response as he was married. I said that I needed them but he took the package out of my pack. The next day "the expected" happened on the climb, and it was a disgusting experience to use socks instead of tampons. I can't believe I was so timid that I allowed him to do that to me!

We endured a stormy night with heavy rainfall while huddling under an overhang. I don't understand why being very uncomfortable and footsore is such a delight. The sudden and intense storm caused a flash flood in the creek-bed that we were following, and we were almost washed away. When we came down from the mountains we headed for a coastal town with beautiful sandy beaches. The physicists and mathematicians in our group spent an entire day devising ways to calculate the "angle of repose" of the sand without any measuring instruments or log tables. Their amazing feat was to calculate it to the exact correct angle by deriving log tables, written on the sand, and other theoretical calculations. The calculations were correct. I recall that the angle of repose was 58 degrees.

Starting a Family

We decided that it was time to start a family, even though I hadn't yet finished my graduate work. I thought I would be finished soon with my research. I was wrong about that, but soon enough, there was a baby on the way, planned for September, so that I could deliver the baby between the summer session and the start of the fall semester. Our little one-bedroom cottage seemed too small for a family, so we started hunting for a larger home without much luck, because but no landlord was willing to rent to people with children.

Hugh suggested that we should buy a house, but I felt that we couldn't afford it, and I had no background in home repairs or gardening. Hugh won the argument. I called a realtor who had a list of three houses that we could look at. Just like *Goldilocks and the Three Bears*, the first cottage was too small, the second house was too expensive, and the third was just right. Unfortunately, it was near the top of the Berkeley Hills where there was no bus service, and I couldn't drive. I felt so guilty for spending about two hours of the realtor's time that I agreed to buy 144 Fairlawn Drive, a shabby three-bedroom house where I still live—although we have remodeled it extensively. The price was twenty-one thousand dollars, outrageously high then, laughably low today. The inside of the house was dark and gloomy and was painted a hideous institutional green. The linoleum floors and counter tops and drapes were all this same bilious color. I think Sears must have made billions of gallons of green paint, decorating every mid-century houses the same ghastly color.

We moved into our new house two weeks before our baby was due, and with the help of friends, we painted and fixed up as much as we could before the delivery date. We had no phone service, and there was no bus service. I had to hitchhike up and down the hill to go to campus. I had no trouble getting rides, since I was obviously pregnant, and drivers took pity on me and gave me lifts. People were compassionate and eagerly gave me rides to campus, but it was harder getting rides going back home. I had an easy and uneventful pregnancy and was able to hike, bicycle and go Israeli folk dancing the entire nine months.

Fortunately, I went into labor on a Saturday evening when Hugh was at home, and he was able to drive me to Alta Bates hospital to give birth. I hadn't thought about how to get to the hospital during the time that Hugh was at work in Livermore, and I had no phone to call a cab. I can't believe how naïve I was. We got to the hospital at 11:00 pm. I had already started labor and was three hours along, but we waited in the parking lot for the day to change to Sunday to avoid paying for an extra night at the hospital. We saved a whole day's cost by avoiding checking in on Saturday, only one hour before midnight. Health insurance did not pay for maternity and delivery costs then, because pregnancy was "not an illness." Fortunately, things have changed, and most insurance policies now include maternity costs.

Our First Baby, Ralph

When I checked into the hospital, the new maternity nurse on duty told me that I wasn't in labor and that Hugh should go home. I didn't realize that this was a ruse to get rid of fathers who would be "in the way" during labor, or worse, faint. As soon as Hugh left, I went into hard labor. It was obvious to me that there wasn't much progress in the labor, and I spent a difficult, scary and lonely night in unbelievable discomfort.

There was a change of shifts at 6:00 AM. and I asked the new nurse to call the doctor. Dr. Aitken, whom we had picked, because his name was first in the alphabetical list of obstetricians in the phonebook, and his office was close by our home. Dr. Aitken found that the baby was in "transfer arrest" with a shoulder presenting. He spent a lot of time trying to turn the baby so that the head would present first. Eventually he used a procedure called "high forceps delivery" and went "fishing" with the forceps to grasp the head. This was a very uncomfortable and painful procedure that is fortunately no longer used. The baby was turned by Dr. Aitken, but he presented in the posterior position, so the delivery was still slow and painful. Eventually a baby boy was born with huge forceps marks on his cone-shaped head. Dr. Aitken reassured me that the marks would disappear and that the baby would have a normal head shape. We now had a beautiful and healthy little boy, whom we named Ralph which means "healer" in Hebrew. I was euphoric and wanted to start another baby, ASAP. We brought Ralph home the next day and were incredibly thrilled to have this fantastic baby. Both sets of grandparents were delighted. Hugh adored Ralph and announced his arrival to anyone who would listen. He climbed the roof of our former cottage where our good friends, the Konrad's still lived, and yelled out the good news to the whole neighborhood.

The wooden toilet seat in the bathroom of our new house was really disgusting, so Hugh tried to do a good deed—he painted it. Unfortunately, he chose "outdoor" varnish, which took a week to dry, so I wasn't able to use the toilet when I got home. Hugh had expected me to stay in the hospital for three days and that the painted seat would be dry by that time, but it wasn't. I was released from the hospital shortly after Ralph's birth, so I had to trot my sore behind down to the basement, where we had another bathroom. Going up and down the stairs ended up therapeutic for my healing.

We planned to have a Bris (Jewish circumcision) for Ralph, so I immediately set about arranging for a Mohel and a Minyan for the event. We invited ten men for the Minyan, and I went to work, baking for the guests. We continued to clean up our new "fixer-upper" home for our first visitors. One of the ten men, Livermore physicist Dr. Ray Fox, fainted during the circumcision and fell to the ground. I was worried that the Bris wasn't Kosher, since there were only nine male witnesses who were conscious. I later discovered that a *Minyan*, (quorum of ten men) isn't required for a Bris. It should have been obvious to me, because our forefather, Abraham, had circumcised himself alone. It makes me feel faint to think about it. I had received some good advice from a friend who told me to have a stiff brandy before the cutting and nurse the baby soon afterward. "The alcohol will make the baby drowsy, and he will fall asleep instantly "she said. I followed that good advice and it worked.

When Ralph was six weeks old, in November of 1959, we joined some friends to go camping in Yosemite at the Sierra Club high country lodge. There were several couples with babies, and we nursed our babies together, drank hot buttered rum, and froze in the unheated cabin. Someone had forgotten the butter, so we used oleo margarine instead – it became a new recipe which we named "Hot Oleoed Rum." How foolish we all were, but we had fun, sang and hiked. I can't imagine doing that now. We are all still good friends and our kids and even grandkids are all grown up. The babies were all great fun for us, and we had quite a nursery of future climbers.

Back to Graduate Work

I found that taking care of Ralph was exciting and satisfying, but I was committed to finishing my graduate work. A few weeks after the birth, I went back to the lab, leaving pumped milk for the feedings I would miss. We had a very nice baby sitter who cared lovingly for Ralph but neglected housework. This worked well, except that hitchhiking to campus was exhausting. My only problem was my extreme fatigue, because Ralph woke up frequently during the nights. Hugh was very helpful in bringing Ralph to me so that I could nurse him in bed, after which Hugh would diaper him and put him back in his crib. In the morning, I would say that the baby had slept through the night, but Hugh would correct me, saying that actually he had nursed twice. Hugh was a fabulous dad.

Hugh's Father's Passing in 1960

When Ralph was nine months old, we received a terrifying phone call that Hugh's father was choking and that we needed to come to Palo Alto immediately. Hugh's father, Charles, was already dead by the time we arrived. His carotid artery had suddenly burst, and it was all over quickly. We were grateful that he did not suffer, but Charles was only 57 years old and seemed much too young and energetic to die. Hugh and I were happy that Charles lived long enough to see his new grandson. Charles had been active as a volunteer on the Palo Alto police force and the entire force as well as the Palo Alto city council accompanied the hearse to the cemetery. It was a great tribute to a citizen who had volunteered much of his time to community service. My uncle Max passed away a few months later. These were huge losses for us, so soon after starting our own family.

Summers in Boulder

Hugh was invited to teach a physics course in Boulder, Colorado, for an annual summer physics graduate program. I had the summer off from teaching, so we drove to Boulder and stayed at the dorms for a month. The invitation was renewed each subsequent summer, so we had a marvelous opportunity to enjoy the Rocky Mountains at no cost. We had meals at the dormitory, so I was freed from cooking and so enjoyed a really wonderful vacation hiking with Ralph in my baby backpack. We made many friends among the other families attending the conference. We took many trips hiking and picnicking in the mountains with the other faculty members and students.

Baby Ralph enjoyed the dorms where he had lots of companions to play with. The only problem was that Ralph, who was now crawling, picked up and ate cigarette butts. The summer dorm residents (not the physicists, but the teachers and sociologists) littered our dorm with butts. Ralph became violently sick, and I discovered the expelled butts in his poop. Fortunately, Ralph recovered quickly, and I stopped him from crawling around the area by the dorms.

When Ralph was seven months old, and I was lying on our

bed nursing him, our cat, also named Hugh (short for Sir Hugh Foot, diplomat and governor of Cyprus,) jumped up onto the bed dragging what looked like a long pink string behind him. I was horrified to realize that the string was the remnant of the unravelling of one of his testicles. When Hugh returned home, I asked him to take the cat to the vet in order to take care of the situation. The vet recommended that the poor cat should be "fixed," i.e. castrated, and I said, "absolutely not!' The vet removed the unraveled side and left the good side, which eventually migrated to the center. A few months later the cat disappeared, so I placed an ad in a local newspaper, to report the missing cat. When the editor asked if there were any distinguishing characteristics I reported that the cat had only one ball and that it was in the center, under the tail. The newspaper said that they couldn't put that into the ad. Unfortunately, we never saw the cat again.

Second Baby, Joel

We returned to Berkeley at the end of August 1960, and I
resumed my graduate work and started another baby. This time
I was determined to have some more time at home after the
birth, so we planned for an August birth. Joel Nathan – "God
Given"—arrived at Alta Bates on August 13, 1961. We were
listening to the radio during the labor and found out that the
Berlin Wall was erected separating East and West Germany. Joel
was a gorgeous and healthy baby, like Ralph. He was very fat
and frantically wanted to eat all of the time. It took both Hugh
and me to feed him, one of us putting the food into his mouth
while and the other was filling the next spoonful. I was lucky
that I finished my graduate work just before he was born, so he
could nurse constantly without my having leave for the lab. I
was able to take off for two months before resuming my job in
the bacteriology department. The two little boys were quite a
handful. One baby slept most of the day and was up at night,
and the other had the opposite schedule; so there was no sleep
for the parents.

Driver's License

Living in the Berkeley Hills without being able to drive was not working. I decided to learn how to drive Pepperl and become independent of buses and hitchhiking. I had already started to learn to drive on our trip in rural Yugoslavia, but I managed to hit two chickens running across the road in opposite directions. Their slaughter made me so sick that I resolved to never drive again. Hugh thought that it was funny, but I was devastated. I was forced to re-assess my decision when I had two babies, so Hugh, my driving instructor, took me to the abandoned Livermore Laboratory airport to teach me how to drive in the absence of any traffic or chickens. I drove around, starting, stopping, turning and backing up, until an official Livermore Lab security guard stopped us and questioned why I was driving around in circles at the airport. We explained what was happening, and he laughed and after warning us that driving on the tarmac was illegal, left us alone.

I passed my driving test and acquired a driver's license. I could now shop and take the babies to the pediatrician by car. But I am still afraid to drive on freeways. My reaction time and distance judgment are poor and avoiding the freeway limits both social events and job opportunities. I am afraid of causing accidents by misjudging distances or getting distracted. Hugh always did the freeway driving, and I only drove on relatively short trips to and from work, the pediatrician's office and the grocery store. This fear still has had an impact on my mobility, but at least I haven't killed anyone.

Our Pets

We have always had pets, both cats and dogs, at the same time. Our first cat was adopted as a kitten when we lived in our cottage on Ellsworth Street. We were smitten with our kitten and we brought her (she turned out to be a male when he eventually developed his balls) to our new house on Fairlawn. He was very jealous when we bought the crib, which he rightly assumed was going to belong to our new baby. I had bought some diapers and was advised to wash them before using them to get rid of the lint. I then stored the diapers in the crib and soon discovered that our cat had pooped on the diapers. "So much for your new baby. POOP!"

Shortly after the loss of the cat, we adopted a fat dachshund, named Banana, from friends who were moving to Pakistan. Banana was a ridiculous, but affectionate, dog who accepted our new kitten, a female. The two animals were good friends and tolerated, and even liked, our baby. The new cat soon became a mother, and we had four more kittens, one of which founded a long line of cats for our family. Banana succumbed eventually, and we adopted a golden retriever puppy named Machismo, whom we called Machi for short. Machi was an Olympian athlete, full of mischief and had boundless energy. He once swam about 30 miles from Iowa City to Cedar Rapids, where he was dragged out of the water by some fraternity students. One of the students phoned us, so Hugh drove to Cedar Rapids where Machi was sitting on a couch watching TV with some fraternity members who were drinking beer. It was a very funny sight. We were in Iowa City where Hugh spent a Sabbatical year in the physics department

Machi was always getting into trouble, and his picture even landed on the front page of the *Des Moines Register* (the Iowa City paper). He ate everything, including a "nerf" ball, a darning needle, a sock and several other objects, and he had to have surgery several times to remove the objects. He was a squirrel chaser and once knocked himself unconscious by running into a tree while chasing a squirrel. Machi was an escape artist and a water dog, and I had frequent phone calls from people who wanted me to come and get him out of their swimming pool. Machi once impaled himself on a stick, and his abdomen was injured and filled with air. He was stitched up by our vet, but we had to manage the crepitation from his belly for weeks. One day I received a call from the Lawrence Hall of Science saying that Machi was in their nature pond and I needed to come and get him before he destroyed the ecology of the pond. What a rascal! Our next dog, named Aristotle, also a golden retriever, (actually Ralph's dog) and our two Bernese mountain dogs, Lolita and Serena, were much mellower and didn't get into much trouble, even though they were physically enormous, weighing about 120 pounds. I adored having pets because they never criticized or teased me, were loving, loyal and gentle, and I felt safe with them.

Fulbright to India and Around-the-World Trip (1963)

Hugh received a Fulbright fellowship to teach at the Madras (now Chennai) Institute for Mathematical Studies in 1963, the year of the Cuban Missile Crisis and the Kennedy assassination. I was reluctant to spend a year in India with two young children and to give up my position in the UC Berkeley bacteriology department, but the chance to have an exotic adventure was irresistible. It seemed reasonable that we should take a year leave from Berkeley before Ralph and Joel started school, rather than interrupting their education. I wasn't aware of the challenges that accompanied traveling around the world with a two-year-old and a four-year-old.

FBI Interrogation

After Hugh applied for our passports we received a phone call from the FBI for him to come for an "Informal" interview and bring a lawyer. This was during the height of the McCarthy era, when the US government harassed people whom they thought were Communist sympathizers. Hugh dutifully went to the "interview" without an attorney and found that the FBI was

136

concerned about a petition he had signed about ending nuclear testing. He was ultimately granted a passport but it showed us how politically vulnerable we were.

Hugh flew to Washington, DC, to participate in the Fulbright orientation program, that coincided with the "March on Washington For Jobs and Freedom," so he was able to hear Dr. Martin Luther King Jr.'s famous "I Have A Dream" speech, at government expense. A month later we started our trip with a flight to Hawaii where we spent two days in Honolulu while Hugh gave lectures at the University. A friendly member of the University of Hawaii's physics department hosted us giving me two restful days at the beach with Joel and Ralph. We continued our travels to Japan where we spent a month at the invitation of the University in Tokyo. We were greeted graciously by the physics department, and I was accompanied daily by a student who showed Joel, Ralph and me around while Hugh was lecturing. We received a gift every morning from the Physics department, and I was tremendously impressed by the department's hospitality and generosity.

Tokyo

We stayed at an elegant hotel in Tokyo, and the kids enjoyed the communal bath that was shared by the other hotel residents. One day I noticed that the water level in the bath was starting to go down, and I was horrified to discover that Joel had removed the stopper from the drain. I tried to replace the stopper but couldn't find the mouth of the drain, so I rushed the kids out of the bath and returned to our room, and hoped that no one would discover that we were responsible. The boys were full of energy back in our room. They raced around and crashed into an elegantly painted screen. I was terrified that we would be held responsible for these accidents, and I prayed we wouldn't cause any more destruction.

I accompanied Hugh to the physics institute one day, taking along the two boys. We sat in the seminar room where Hugh gave a lecture titled "The Perturbation Theory Derivation of the Debye-Huckel Plasma Energy." This is the only lecture title that I bothered to memorize, and I didn't understand a single word of it. The boys sat quietly, mesmerized by watching their father deliver a lecture to a large audience. We never attended any more of his physics lectures.

We traveled comfortably by train to Kyoto, Mount Fuji, Nagoya and many other scenic places. The food was excellent, the sleeping accommodations were fabulous, and the people were courteous and friendly. Our only negative experience was on our last day in Tokyo while I was packing our bags and bringing them to the checkout desk. While I was in the lobby checking out, all our money was stolen from our room. I had waited for the last minute to change our yen (the compensation for Hugh's month of teaching) into dollars. And now it was gone. There was no time to call the police, so I notified the hotel of the theft and arrived at the airport penniless. It was embarrassing to arrive in Hong Kong without any money, but the US Embassy helped us get through this ordeal by issuing travelers' checks on our American account. About two years later, back in the States, we received a letter from the Tokyo police who had captured the thief, and we were reimbursed fully for the amount that was stolen.

There was a drought in Hong Kong during our stay, and the mainland Chinese had turned off the piped water into the province, so the only available water was what was pumped from ships in the port. There was no water for showers or laundry, and we accumulated a week's worth of dirty diapers from the incessant diarrhea the boys got in Asia. On our last night, I packed up the soiled diapers into suitcases (I was afraid there might not be any diapers available in India or else I would have abandoned the dirty ones – how silly I was) and we flew to Calcutta *via* Singapore.

The flight to Calcutta was long and tiring, and the boys ran out of patience with their books and puzzles, so we allowed them to play on the floor by our seats. I ran out of entertainment for the boys, and they had a hard time dealing with the long flight. We finally landed in India only to endure another two hour wait trapped in our seats while the plane was disinfected, a routine procedure. It was hot, uncomfortable, and I quickly regretted our Indian adventure.

Arrival in Calcutta

It was stifling hot in the plane and the diapers were starting to stink and emit ammonia, but we endured the long flight and the endless inspections on the arrival in Calcutta. The Fulbright agent who was to meet us was prevented from rushing us through the arrival procedures, and the inefficiency of inspecting our incoming luggage was a disaster. It took several hours to get through all the paperwork, in quintuplicate and without carbon paper, until we were allowed to enter India. What made it worse was that an insect had crawled into Hugh's ear, and buzzed for a long time before it died. Hugh almost went insane from the loud buzzing in his ear. Our attempt to drown the insect failed. The drive from the airport to the Grand Hotel took several more hours because of the cattle and the homeless people who were on the roads, so we arrived at the hotel late at night. After putting the boys to sleep, I decided to wash the dirty diapers of their contents in the bathtub in our suite. Another disaster! The bathtub drain was plugged and, you guessed it, the tub ended up full of poop. I was mortified, and I refused to allow the porter to enter and take our suitcases to our taxi when we left. I wanted to dash out ASAP.

In the morning I decided to take the boys for a walk in the street while waiting for the taxi, but there was a huge demonstration, with thousands of screaming participants charging through the streets. The demonstrators had sticks and clubs and the situation looked extremely dangerous, so we stayed in the hotel lobby. My naïve ideas of a peaceful and passive India evaporated. I don't know what the demonstrations were all about, but there was a war going on between India and China, over Kashmir, and it might have been related to that. The issues were probably wages or housing, but I never found out. Anti-War demonstrations in Berkeley were tame compared to what I saw in Calcutta. I was disappointed that Gandhi's strategy of "Passive Resistance" was not being implemented. The Grand Hotel had a large courtyard that was full of exotic plants and colorful birds, so the boys and I passed an enjoyable time waiting for the taxi, without having to go out into the street.

To Madras

We took a taxi to the airport and discovered that the wet and dirty diapers, reeking of ammonia, caused our luggage to be overweight, and we had to pay a fortune to board the plane. The flight to Madras was on a propeller plane, and it seemed to take an eternity. We eventually arrived and got to a hotel, with the dirty diapers. I was relieved to finally arrive at our destination after six weeks of travel, and I tried to relax at our hotel until we found a place to rent for the academic year.

The Math-Science Institute had a list of available housing, and I did a search while Hugh was checking into the institute and his office. Most of the apartments or houses were far too fancy for us and were appropriate for embassy personnel who needed a staff of servants. I decided on the upper flat of duplex residence on Ritherdon Road, in the Vepery district, with an Indian family living downstairs. I thought it would be interesting to live in close contact with the Indian family, and the bonus was that Ralph and Joel had two young boys and two dogs, Pickles and Samba, to play with.

Our new upstairs flat had not yet been completed nor occupied because India was at war with China, the 1962 Sino-Indian Border Conflict. All building materials had been confiscated for the war effort. Private buildings were not completed until after the end of hostilities, since cement had been requisitioned for the war effort. All civilian construction was halted. We had two bedrooms, a large living room, a dining room and a "kitchen" which was outside in the courtyard. The bathroom had a shower, but no shower stall, and the water simply splashed down into a drain in the floor. Each room had a huge fan, which could not begin to cool us from the intense heat. The windows had bars to keep out monkeys and birds, but no glass, and crows flew in to eat the food on the table. We put wicker baskets over all of the food to keep it from being eaten by the wildlife. The kitchen had no oven, but it had a type of camping stove with only one burner and a metal box that could be placed over the burner to serve as an oven. Only one item could be cooked at a time. The sink had a drain in one corner from which the water flowed onto the sloping ground to the drain, so I had to go into the kitchen barefoot. The stove was supplied with gas by a propane tank that had no gauge, so I never knew when it was empty. I just had to wait until the flame went out and then order a new tank (we had no phone) that sometimes took days to arrive by oxcart.

Servants

The institute offered to find me servants, so I interviewed an Indian butler who had previously worked for the British Embassy. He informed me that he wanted to hire several more servants who would work under him: an indoor sweeper, an outdoor sweeper, a gardener, a cook, a kitchen cleaner, a toilet cleaner (untouchable) and a nanny. I didn't consider hiring him and the huge staff that he demanded. I hired a cook who spoke no English and had no concept of using a gas stove. I tried to show her how to turn off the gas, but she always blew out the flame and left the gas on. I told her that she had to boil the drinking water but, since she failed to understand the purpose, she would boil the water until the container was dry and then refill it with more un-boiled water. I finally had to dismiss her, but I felt so guilty that I paid her an extra month's wages. Unfortunately, she interpreted that to mean was that she was "hired" to come for one more month. I could do nothing to prevent her from coming daily. I was told that in order to fire her I needed to slap her, but that was something I could not do. I finally hired a nanny/cook who knew a bit of English, but she was used to the British class system. She insisted on squatting in the courtyard, even in the monsoon rains, and wouldn't come into the living room. I finally went out to squat in the rain beside her, and she felt embarrassed and reluctantly came in with me. She was a wonderful person, but she treated the little boys as though they were princes and thoroughly spoiled them. They would command her, "Ayah, fetch me a glass of water," with no "please or "thank you." I feared that their attitude would continue back home.

Ralph and Joel became tired of vegetarian curry after a week in the hotel, so I promised them an American-style meal as soon as the gas tank for the stove was installed. I took the boys to the local outdoor market to buy a chicken, and I was surprised that all of the chickens were ALIVE. I bought some other items, which took several more trips to the market because the various foods were all brought in by farmers from the fields at different times of day. I managed to get the squawking and flapping chicken, and the boys, back to the house and let the chicken go loose in the kitchen. Now what? How to kill the chicken? I couldn't bring myself to do it, so I asked the cook of the downstairs family to do the deed. He was happy to accommodate for receiving the head, neck, organs and feet. Now all I had to do was pluck the feathers and bake it. The poor bird was very thin. I didn't know that I needed to feed the chicken for about a week in order to fatten it up. How naive could I be?

It took two hours to bake the chicken on the improvised stove. After the chicken, came the vegetables, then at last, the rice, all taking turns on the single burner. I finally had the meal prepared before Hugh came home, and I was very proud of myself for having managed to overcome all of the obstacles. I brought the food inside to our dining table and Hugh, who felt very hot and sweaty after having ridden home from the Math Institute on his bicycle, turned on the ceiling fan to help himself cool off. The fan had not been used since its installation, and we didn't realize that geckos had nested on the blades. The poor lizards were flung off and chopped up by the blades and the parts rained down onto our meal. I was terribly upset and screamed that I wanted to go back home to Berkeley. I threw the whole dinner out and we went to a restaurant. I made Hugh clean off the blades and bloody table and forbade him to turn on the fan ever again.

Our host was Professor Alladi Ramakrishnan, founder and director of the Institute of Mathematical Sciences in Madras (now Chennai), and son of one of the writers of the Indian constitution. Professor Ramakrishnan was a kind and hospitable host and invited us to many events at his luxurious home. A few days after we arrived, he invited us to a lavish dinner to which he had invited many dignitaries. There was marvelous food and musical entertainment, and the guests, some of whom were government ministers, were friendly and welcoming. They were charmed by our blond little boys who were dashing around making mischief. The men wore traditional dress including the dhoti, a wrap-around garment that reveals their hairy legs, which intrigued the boys. The women were dressed in gloriously colored silk saris and looked very elegant. Indians adore children and were very tolerant and indulgent of our boys.

Monkeys

A very comical incident happened to us when we planned a picnic in a wood near Madras. We stationed ourselves beneath a tree for shade, and I unpacked sandwiches, boiled eggs, bananas and some chips, and we settled down on a blanket to eat. In a flash, a group of monkeys ran down from the tree and grabbed our food. They chattered in the branches and dropped eggshells and fruit peels on our heads, and then pooped on us. The kids were thrilled by the monkeys, but I was disgusted. Picnics in Berkeley were never like this.

Ear and nose piercing were very common in Madras, so I decided to get some earrings and have my ears pierced, which was free with the purchase of the earrings. A street vendor on one of the main market streets had an extensive display of lovely earrings, so I bargained with him to buy a pair and also pierce my ears. This soon attracted a huge crowd of people, including snake charmers, acrobats, and many colorful merchants and my earring man started to get ready for the piercing, but I hesitated because he wasn't sterilizing the needle. He was puzzled by what I wanted so I went off to a neighboring pharmacy and asked to buy a bottle of alcohol. The clerk informed me that Madras was a dry state and I needed to have a prescription. I decided to buy some matches instead and went back to the earring vendor. I flamed the pin and hoped for the best, but the vendor took the pin and wiped it on his dhoti—the cloth that was wrapped around his groin and legs and into which he blew his nose—and started the piercing. I desperately wanted to back out, but we were now encircled by hundreds of people who were watching. There was no way I could back out, so I held my breath and went through with the procedure. I told my landlady, Rupee, about my experience and she doubled over laughing. I didn't develop an infection and I still have the earrings, and they bring back the memory each time I wear them.

Indian Nursery School

We were lucky to live next door to a teachers' college, and we enrolled Ralph and Joel in their nursery school. The teachers were gentle, spoke some English and were delighted to have the little American boys in their classrooms. They played games and sang songs, and our boys soon acquired South Indian accents. The books were donated by British schools, and were full of the most inappropriate stories to which the Indian children couldn't relate. I recall one illustrated story about Christmas in London with snow, SNOW!, falling outside. The children had no idea what snow was, and all of the elements of the story were strange and unknown to them, however Ralph and Joel enjoyed their nursery school.

Our Madras Neighborhood

Our compound was next to a big pond, called a tank, which was full of snakes, and Water Buffalo. The buffalo were submerged so deeply in the pond that only their horns and noses showed above the surface. I was very worried about snakes crawling into our house, but my downstairs Indian neighbor, Rupee, assured me that there was a mongoose family on the property, which would catch the snakes before they could get into the bushes around the house. I was inclined to believe her as she was even closer to the pond than I was, and she didn't seem worried. There were lots of mosquitoes, so we slept under mosquito nets because we were concerned about malaria. When we got into bed we spent the first ten minutes killing mosquitoes. Inevitably, there was always one mosquito left, that continued to buzz around maddeningly. We all took anti-malaria pills and quinine every day.

The US embassy informed us that it wasn't safe to buy milk from street vendors because many cows were infected with tuberculosis. I bought/rented a healthy, inspected cow and had her owner come and milk her twice a day in our patio. His pay was only a few rupees, plus some of her milk, which I shared with the downstairs family. I had a vet check the cow for TB and she was deemed healthy, but I still heated the milk on our little stove to pasteurize it. I bought a tiny refrigerator, the largest I could find, which was delivered by ox cart. There was barely enough room in it for the milk and for the beer that Hugh brought home on his bicycle. Madras was a "dry" state but foreigners could obtain a license to purchase small amounts of beer. Hugh couldn't stand the heat and insisted he needed cold beer in order to function.

Lepers and Beggars

A family infected with of leprosy were camped on the road right by our house, and I had to pass by them whenever I left or entered. They were very pitiful, so I frequently gave them food and money. I was told to stop doing that because it interfered with their motivation to go for treatment. The more pitiful they looked, the better they could beg, so they didn't want their sores treated. It was very difficult for me to pass by without giving. One day while I was walking on the street a pair of lepers started to beg from me. I did not give them money, so one of them put his mutilated hand down my blouse and rubbed me. I knew from my bacteriology classes that it is difficult to transmit leprosy unless there are open wounds, so I tolerated their attack.

We were close to the magnificent Madras beach, and we frequently strolled there in the evening after the heat of the day. The sandy beach, seven miles long, was filled with people enjoying the cool evenings after the heat of the day. There were food and jewelry vendors, fishermen and their families resting by their boats, beggars, tourists and cows all crowded on the sand. It felt like a carnival and it was fun. We saw two young women students from the Math Institute one evening walking with some male students, not their relatives. They were seen by some Institute faculty and were expelled the next day, but the male students were not expelled.

Our Trips In India

Were took several trips to ancient monuments and small villages and were able to explore the countryside by taking taxis. The taxis were old and some had no dashboards, and in some cases the drivers had to manually connect wires to start the engine. Many drivers drove extremely slowly, probably to avoid cows, so their engines did not get charged. Many of the villages had looms in the streets, for villagers to weave colorful saris. The looms were very long, and would never have fit into their houses.

I was amazed to see how primitive the irrigation systems were in the fields. They were operated by men who walked back and forth on a seesaw pump. One man walked back and forth on the seesaw, while the other man took the full bucket and carried it out into the field. It seemed very tiring and inefficient, but that was the custom and it worked.

We saw a sad sight in one village where a housing facility was filled with young women who were crippled and sat in wheelchairs. These women, girls really, had jumped into wells in order to escape from arranged marriages and brutal mothers-in-law and had not succeeded in committing suicide. It was a pathetic and disturbing sight. The women were cared for by Christian missionaries who were very kind and caring.

Hugh and I took several long trips by train to other cities, such as Bangalore, and to wildlife preserves. Travel by rail in India is beyond description. The fellow passengers were packed in with their wares and livestock. We had met an Australian couple who needed a place to stay because their ship was delayed in the Madras port. We allowed them to camp in our yard. We asked them to baby-sit while we took a trip without the boys. We travelled by train to Bangalore and then by a taxi to a game lodge, where we tracked wild animals while riding on an elephant. Riding an elephant was definitely one of my most exotic experiences, but I was disappointed that we didn't see any wild animals, probably because we were making too much noise. When we returned to the lodge, I was offered a wild ocelot kitten—it was adorable, but what could I do with it? I don't believe in trying to make pets out of wild animals and felt very sorry for the ocelot kitten.

On the way home on the train Hugh developed a terrible infection on his foot, which was turning black. It was an emergency, and we disembarked at a stop in a city that had a modern hospital. He received treatment there and luckily didn't have to have an amputation. It was a very scary incident, but it ended happily although Hugh limped for several weeks.

Kennedy Assassination

We were awakened on November 22nd, 1963, by crowd of people who came by to offer condolences to us for the loss of our president, John. F. Kennedy. We had neither radio nor television, and we had not yet heard the news of the assassination. We were shocked and horrified at the murder of our president. We attended a hastily arranged meeting at the US embassy where we were informed about the Dallas shooting. The entire group of Fulbright fellows and other Americans who were in Madras were present, and we were terrified about the consequences of the assassination. It felt very strange and worrisome to be away from home at such a tragic and terrible time.

Living in Madras

Hugh spent most of the time at the Mathematics Institute where he was teaching, while I was coping with running our household and taking care of the boys. I often took them to the Gymkhana Club, which had a wonderful pool and sports facilities. Most of the men at the club were boozy British retired bureaucrats who avoided the pool and hung out at the bar drinking whiskey all afternoon. I was the only person there with children. It was very pleasant at the club, and the boys enjoyed splashing around in the cool water. The club was restricted to British (non-Indian) people, so there were no other Americans for me to visit with. Our family had obtained a special pass through the courtesy of the Math-Science Institute, and I frequently took advantage of it. It was either too hot or too rainy to take the boys for walks during the monsoon, so I spent time visiting with our downstairs neighbor, Rupee, and her two sons who were about the same ages as Ralph and Joel, or we visited an American Fulbright neighbor who also had two young sons. We spent our time drinking tea and discussing politics or Indian customs. Our landlady was divorced from her diplomat husband and lived with her mother. She was terrified of her former husband and was afraid that he would abduct the boys, his legal right, so she kept them indoors or at school much of the time.

I hosted many foreign visitors who came for short stays at the Math-Sci Institute. It was a wonderful opportunity to meet people from Ireland, France, Israel, Italy and Australia, and we made life-long friendships with many of them. The Institute guests were very happy to have a home-cooked European style meal during their stay at hotels in Madras. Most "upper class" restaurants had only vegetarian menus, and I was able to prepare meals with fish or chicken for our guests.

We went to the movies occasionally and saw Indian and foreign films. Madras was the film capitol of India at the time, and I was able to visit the studios and meet with some of the actors. Indian films had the unusual custom of inserting a musical-dance interlude whether or not it seemed appropriate. Foreign films were strictly censored, and sexual scenes and murders were edited out. It was strange to see "Macbeth" without any of the murders, and the film made no sense in its cut form. There was always a short film about the war with China, with a warning not to give away military secrets such as train schedules. The theaters were hot and stuffy, and the audience was mostly men because unaccompanied women could not go out alone, and there was no "dating" at that time in Madras. I am sure things have changed great deal since we were there. I was privileged to attend several South Indian musical dance concerts, which were amazing. The instrumentalists were great, and the dances were beautiful and mysterious. The concerts were very long, and I was rarely able to sit through the full three-hour performances.

Leaving Madras and the Final
Fulbright Conference

The end of our stay in Madras came in March 1964, just at the start of extremely hot weather. We arose at about 3:00 AM on the morning of our departure and found that both of our boys were very sick. They could hardly walk and had fevers. We had no choice but to take a taxi to the airport with our two sick kids and board the plane. As soon as we were on the plane I saw that they had swollen necks and realized that they had the mumps, although they had been vaccinated. It must have been a different strain of the mumps virus from the vaccination, because Hugh and I also got the mumps about a week later, even though we both had the disease as children. Our poor kids suffered through the flight and during the narrow-track train trip up a steep mountain where our final Fulbright conference was held. The other families at the conference were frightened that their kids would catch the mumps, and so we had to isolate our boys from most of the activities. The three-day conference was held at a mountaintop resort, that was blissfully cool. Hugh managed to bring the food from the dining hall to our room, where I was isolated with the boys. There were lectures and reports from the other Fulbright fellows and we learned a great deal about India and its social and political problems. Some of the Fulbright students were of the "counter culture" type, and it was embarrassing to see emissaries of the US with straggly long hair and ragged clothes. It seemed to me that they were mocking the poor people in India, but they were just members of the counter-culture.

Anaphylactic Shock in Response to Mangoes

We flew to the metropolis of Mumbai (Bombay) on the west coast of India where our friends, Kalyani and Kirit Pandya, had relatives. We had met Kalyani and Kirit in Berkeley, where they had been graduate students. We stayed at the apartment of Kalyani's mother, who was the director of a large engineering firm. Mumbai is a port city with a huge harbor, and it has an extremely varied and dense population. (The population in 2016 was estimated at 22 million.) The city has a mixture of many cultures, faiths, cuisines and languages including Hindi, English, and Urdu. It is an exciting city with fine arts and festivals, and is home to persons of varied professional social and political identities. In 1960, the State was split along linguistic lines, but Mumbai, then called Bombay, subsequently embarked on a decade of cultural boom.

One afternoon we had a fabulous lunch at the home of our Indian friends, we were served the first mangoes of the season. Our hosts then took us out for a walk in the exciting city of Bombay. Hugh enjoyed eating the mangoes but, shortly afterwards, he looked at me and pointed to his face. His tongue was sticking out of his mouth, and he was turning purple. He couldn't speak, because his breathing was impaired, and he started to fall. I remembered from one of my immunology courses that those were the symptoms of anaphylactic shock, and I informed my host, who immediately called her brother who was a medical doctor. He gave Hugh an adrenaline injection and drove us to a clinic where Hugh was given oxygen and treated for high blood pressure. Hugh almost died from his dramatic allergy to a mango. It was a frightening event, but the outcome was good, and Hugh was able to rest and recover.

We wanted to visit the ancient cave temples of Elephanta Island, located in the Mumbai harbor, that I was not allowed to visit. The trip to Elephanta was only for Hugh. The cave temples are dedicated to the Hindu god, Shiva. Hugh was able to visit Elephanta by ferry, but women were not allowed because of the erotic carvings in the temples. This reminded me of the time when we were in Pompeii, where Hugh was allowed to visit a museum that contained 2000-year-old erotica, but I was denied admission.

New Delhi

We travelled to New Delhi, India's capitol, where Hugh had been invited to give several lectures. The boys and I stayed at the hotel where we registered in the morning, while Hugh went to the physics institute to give his lectures. It was not easy trying to keep the boys amused. The hotel's pool had been drained, and I was afraid that our boys, who were running around in the courtyard, would fall into the concrete pool base. Hugh left me with no money, because he had planned to return immediately after a coffee reception for him with the institute's welcoming committee, however he stayed the entire day. It was blazingly hot, and the boys and I had nothing to drink or eat until Hugh returned in the late afternoon. I tried to get food and drink through room service, but the hotel had registered us under the institute's name, which they did not understand represented us. I was so angry and frustrated that when Hugh returned in the evening that I locked myself in the bathroom to avoid him. It was a crazy and childish thing to do, but all I wanted was to go back home to Berkeley and get a divorce.

The Red Fort in Delhi

By the next day I had calmed down and forgiven Hugh, and we planned a trip see the Red Fort located in the northern end of Delhi. The Fort is a World Heritage site that was built as a residence for the Emperor of India in the 1600s. It was completed in 1648, and contains palaces, halls and even a mosque, most of which have now been converted into museums, showcasing the lavish lifestyle of the Mughal Era. The fort and its inner structures gave us a look at the intricacy and accuracy of the architectural style of that era. Some of the structures were in ruins, but they were still grand and impressive.

Agra

We traveled to Agra in Uttar Pradesh, where we visited the Taj Mahal, "Crown of the Palace," one of the Seven Wonders of the World. The Taj Mahal is an ivory-white marble mausoleum, which was commissioned in 1632 by the Mughal emperor, Shah Jahan, to house the tomb of his favorite wife. The mausoleum has minarets, a mosque, beautiful symmetrical gardens, and a long reflecting pool leading up to the entrance of the mosque. The day was intensely hot, and Joel, semi-intentionally, fell into the reflecting pool. I was terrified that we would get arrested, but people just laughed, and we pulled him out, cooled off and happy. The Indians are very tolerant of children, a very good thing for us. After the mango and the pool incidents, I was looking forward to travel without any more problems, however this was not to be. Our next trip destination was Pakistan, which had its own adventures for us.

Our Flight to Pakistan

We flew from India to Karachi, which is the largest and most populous city in Pakistan. We travelled in an old propeller plane over the foothills of the Himalayas and the plane barely cleared the mountains. The flight was extremely bumpy and the plane took leaps and plunges and Joel got airsick and vomited on the lap of the passenger next to him. The gentleman was extremely gracious about it and the stewardess cleaned things up. A member of the Pakistani Energy Commission drove us to a pre-arranged lodging and helped us settle in. Hugh soon discovered that one side of his face was extremely swollen, with a huge swelling on his neck behind his ear. He had to tilt his head sideways to accommodate the swelling, a "mump" as he called it, but he agreed to deliver his lecture to the Pakistani Atomic Energy Commission. Hugh was feeling horrible, but managed deliver his lecture before collapsing. The boys were recovering from their mumps and were grouchy, demanding and noisy. I soon heard a loud knock on our door and a very grumpy Englishman complained about our noisy boys. I was lost for an effective way of dealing with Ralph and Joel, so I told them that I would call the "Bad Man" from next door if they made any more noise. That terrified them. It was a drastic move, but it worked. Eventually the boys fell asleep and felt much better the next morning. Traveling is hard on kids and I felt really sorry for them but, with a sick husband and two sick boys, I was very stressed.

The Khyber Pass

Our good friends from the Stanford Alpine Club, Joan and Karl Stauffer, the parents of our adopted dog, Banana, and their three young children, were living and working in Peshawar, Pakistan, and invited us to come and stay with them. Karl was a geologist who had a temporary position in Pakistan, and Joan was a teacher at the local American school. We had a wonderful reunion with our friends who insisted that we visit the Khyber Pass that connects Kabul with Peshawar, a place few Americans visited. We needed to get a visa to go to the Khyber Pass, so Hugh tried to arrange for a visa, which was denied. The reason was that another Hugh DeWitt had gone to the pass during the previous week, and the bureaucrats wondered why he would make a second trip so soon. Hugh remembered that there was a Hugh DeWitt who had graduated from Stanford a few years after he did. The other Hugh was a biologist who specialized in marine biology and discovered how icefish could survive the Arctic without freezing. He demonstrated that they had a type of anti-freeze in their blood.

Hugh convinced the bureaucrats that he was a different Hugh DeWitt, and they eventually accepted the explanation. What a coincidence! Two Hugh DeWitts visiting the Khyber Pass within just a few days! Our friend, Karl, arranged for a driver, and we drove to the mountain pass connecting Afghanistan and Pakistan, cutting through the northeastern part of the Spin Ghar (Hindu Kush) mountains. The pass goes 33 miles through the Hindu Kush, reaching an elevation of about 3,500 feet. The pass is full of switchbacks, each having a group of caves protected by fierce looking armed men. When we reached the border between Pakistan and Afghanistan, we were approached by a particularly fierce Afghani man who loved the boys and gave Ralph an axe, a hatchet with a spear on one end, which we still have in our living room. The axe had a dent, and the man explained that that it had been used to chop off someone's head. I didn't believe him, but it could be true. The blood had been wiped off. If our State Department had asked me, I would have told them that there was no way we could win the current war with Afghanistan. The people were too fierce, and they knew their territory and all of the caves intimately.

Kashmir

We took a little vacation to Kashmir, where we stayed on a houseboat on a lake near Srinagar. The lake was surrounded by high mountains and was full of houseboats and vendors in little rowboats. The houseboat was quaint, comfortable and very relaxing. We were visited by numerous merchants who sold local food, art, Kashmiri scarves and other lovely objects. I bought a few scarves, and I regret not buying more. We rested up on the houseboat before flying to Iran.

Persia/Iran

Our destination was Israel, but Pakistan and Israel did not have diplomatic relations at that time, so we had to fly to Iran to continue our trip. We flew to Teheran to make our way westward from Iran, over Iraq. When we boarded the plane in Pakistan, Ralph, now 4 1/2 years old, was carrying his axe, but there were no complaints from the stewards. The flight was British, and the pilots invited the boys into the cockpit, just for their entertainment. Ralph was still carrying his axe, but the pilots didn't seem to mind. In terms of today's politics and travel restrictions, it is mind blowing. We stayed at a fancy hotel in Tehran where all of the porters were dwarfs. Our boys were fascinated by the dwarfs, because they were about the same size as they were, but the dwarfs could carry heavy suitcases. I tried to tell the boys to not stare at the porters, but Ralph and Joel were totally intrigued. We only had two days in Tehran, so we limited our sightseeing to the Shah's palace and its surroundings. It seems incredible that, in 2017, ISIS attacked the Iranian parliament in Tehran and the Ayatollah's shrine. We were in Persia during very different times.

The Shah, Mohammad Reza Pahlavi, was a secular Muslim who was overthrown by the Iranian Revolution of February 1979. At the time we were there, we were unaware of any revolutionary movements. The United States backed the Shah at the time, who made efforts to modernize Iran and give the Iranian people a non-Islamic identity. We were astonished by the opulence of the palace, especially the Peacock Throne. The throne, built in the early 17th century, is jeweled, enameled and dazzling.

1964 Flight from Iran to Israel

Our flight path took us over Iraq, but we could not fly over Jordan or Lebanon because of their hostilities with Israel. The flight took us over Syria and then out over the Mediterranean, where our plane made U-turn and approached Israel from the west.

The moment I arrived in Israel I felt at home. It was a strange and unfamiliar feeling, because I had lived in many countries and always felt like a foreigner. I felt accepted and comfortable, even though I couldn't speak Hebrew and didn't know my way around. I felt that no-one challenged my identity, I simply fit in. I had lived in the USA for 18 years and was almost completely Americanized, but I was still part of a minority and I always felt like an outsider. It was wonderful to feel at home.

We arrived just in time for Pesach, but my cousin, whom we planned to visit, had arranged to have a Seder with some friends who were very observant. They were concerned that we might have some breadcrumbs in our pockets, so it wasn't possible for us to enter their home. What about the Mitzvah to ask "all who are hungry to come in and eat" I asked myself? We stayed at a small hotel in Jerusalem and, for the first time in years, didn't celebrate a Seder with family. It seemed ironic after saying, "Next Year in Jerusalem" for so many years, that when we got to Jerusalem, we didn't have a family Seder to attend. The manager of the small hotel in Jerusalem where we were staying was very gracious, and invited us to his Seder. He had no problems with imaginary crumbs. He was kind and hospitable and designed a safe route for us to see as much of Israel as possible.

Our visit to Jerusalem was before the 1967 war and the reunification, so we missed many important sights that we were able to see on later trips. A number of tourists were murdered while we were in Jerusalem, so we were cautious about where we went. We rented a car and drove to, and climbed Masada, the high point of our trip. After Masada, we continued on to Tel Aviv and Herzelia, where my cousins lived.

We made a habit of picking up hitchhiking soldiers who provided entertainment for the boys and were wonderful tour guides. The soldiers went out of their way to show us interesting sites such as Crusader castles, nature preserves, waterfalls and many out-of-the-way sites.

Our visit to some good friends of ours from Berkeley turned out to be sad. The wife, a Holocaust survivor, had committed suicide that very day, so Hugh and I took their three kids for a day trip, so their father could make the funeral arrangement. This tragedy reinforced our understanding why we needed Israel as a haven for the Jews. Not only were 6 million Jews murdered and there were many more who were seriously emotionally damaged-survivors who were never able to recover from their experiences.

Hugh spent three weeks lecturing at the Technion Institute, while I took day trips with the boys. We traveled on the marvelous Israeli bus system, saw a lot and had a great time. We also visited several relatives and friends from Berkeley who had made Aliyah to Israel. The weather was hot and the trips were exhausting, but were interesting and full of history. Our hosts from the Technion were very hospitable, and we had many marvelous meals with them. They all said that they hoped we would return to Israel, perhaps to stay.

Flight to Germany

The Israel visit came to an end, and we flew to Germany where Hugh had a two month-long appointment at the Max Plank Institute for Physics in Garching, near Munich. In the airport I noticed the German symbol of the giant Eagle holding a wreath in its talons, but the wreath itself was empty. During the Nazi time, the wreath held a Swastika in its center. Later, when I told my father about this, he remarked wryly that the wreath was left empty so that the Swastika could be replaced. I felt a chill when I stepped back on German soil.

We had great friends in Garching who had three English speaking children and our boys played with them. The housing assigned to us by the Max Plank Institute was very safe, and the kids were able to play outside in the large court without supervision. We bought a VW bus to tour Europe and shipped it back to Berkeley where it served our family for many years.

Hugh felt comfortable at the Max Plank institute where he revived his German and did research with his colleagues. The boys picked up some German, but we were in Germany for only two months that was not long enough for them to learn how to speak German. We took one marvelous trip to the Alps, but

Hugh was too busy with his lectures to take a long vacation. I felt very stressed with all of the traveling and I wasn't sensitive to Hugh's time demands and I became very irritable.

Germany had changed a lot since our year in 1956. The rubble had been cleared and there was lots of rebuilding. There was not much discussion of the war, but the West Germans were very frustrated with the separation of East and West Germany. Many families were divided and were anxious about the fate of their family members living under the Soviet regime. There was much complaining, but it seemed to us that the West Germans were living rather well.

We visited Dr. Brandt and his family who had been Hugh's host during his 1956 Fulbright year, and they were delighted to see us again. Frau Brandt wasn't well, but she seemed really happy to see us. Sadly, she died shortly afterwards of ovarian cancer. The Brandt boys were now young men and very studious. We made new friends during our stay in Garching, and I am delighted to still be in contact with them.

Belgium, Brussels

At the end of our stay in Garching I had to pack again, and Hugh drove us to Belgium where he had a physics appointment for two months at the Free University in Brussels with Professor Ilya Prigogine. Professor Prigogine, a distinguished physicist and chemist, was appointed director of the International Solvay Institute in Brussels in 1959. He was awarded the 1977 Nobel Prize in Chemistry.

We drove to Brussels *via* Paris and met Hugh's mom at the Paris Airport, and we travelled together to Brussels. The Institute found a very nice apartment for us near a lovely park and fairly close to the Free University. The apartment was charming, but I was depressed at having to set up housekeeping again for the fourth time in a year. Finding schools for the boys, learning how to buy groceries in a French and adapting to local social standards was exhausting. Belgian's were quite strict with children, and our kids were sometimes out of control. The teachers at the school called the boys *"mechant"* which means mischievous. They did not understand that the kids had been traveling for a long time plus couldn't speak French.

Hugh's host, Professor Prigogine, was gracious and

enlivened our stay in Brussels by inviting us on several trips and visits to his home, that was filled with marvelous African art. Professor Prigogine visited us in Berkeley and we were able to reciprocate.

Brussels is a beautiful, international city filled with museums, concert halls, parks and fabulous inexpensive restaurants. We had some amazing meals of many ethnic types. The prices were reasonable, and we took advantage of the restaurants frequently. I took French lessons from a lovely and patient teacher, and was quite proud of myself when I was able to remember my high school French and could build on that. We visited many churches and medieval museums with torture chambers, which fascinated the boys. We visited the Waterloo battlefield where Napoleon was defeated (on June 18,1815). We lived in the French-speaking section of Brussels, but we also visited the Flemish areas. I was quite sad to leave to return to the USA.

While we were in Brussels, on August 5, 1964, we learned of the Gulf of Tonkin disaster involving the unprovoked attack by North Vietnamese torpedo boats on two U.S. ships of the 7th Fleet. President Johnson was given the authority to assist any Southeast Asian country whose government was considered to be jeopardized by "Communist aggression." It seemed very ominous to Hugh and me, and we anticipated an escalation of the Vietnam War, with many casualties, but we were too busy with daily life to spend a lot of time worrying.

Return To USA

We flew back to the US in late August 1964 and were met by my parents met us at La Guardia airport in New York. My mother had forgotten where she parked her car in the huge airport, and we spent several hours searching for it. That was the grand finale of our round-the-world trip. We spent a few days with my parents in Middletown recovering from jet lag and the various minor illnesses that the kids had picked up including worms, mumps and earaches. Our return home to Berkeley was relatively uneventful and we were happy to be home again.

I faced the job of unpacking, placing the boys into appropriate schools and searching for a job. I left the Bacteriology department in 1963 to accompany Hugh on his Fulbright to India without having filed paperwork for a leave of absence, and I found that my former position was no longer available. I postponed job hunting until I had placed the boys into schools and then found out that the job market was virtually closed and nothing was available, so I hurled myself into volunteer activities.

I volunteered in my Synagogue, Congregation Beth El, and was active in the Student Non-Violent Coordinating Committee

(SNCC), which was fighting racial injustice and supporting voter registration for African-Americans. Much of my activity was fundraising for Black voter registration drives but I was expelled, when SNCC rejected white activists, Jews in particular. I was very disappointed by the treatment of Jewish activists by Black civil rights groups and had hoped for a strong coalition of Jews and African Americans, which seemed to be a natural partnership. The rejection hurt but I still supported Black aspirations for equality. Later, I became intensely involved with obtaining US visas for Soviet Jews and attended rallies in front of the Soviet Embassy in San Francisco.

There was a lovely nursery school within walking distance of our house for three-year-old Joel where he spent a wonderful year. Ralph was just shy of being five years old, so I tried to enlist him in public school kindergarten. I was told that he was three weeks too young to start, the cut-off being September 1st, when his birthday was September 20th. I argued with the principal and succeeded in registering Ralph in kindergarten, so he was one year younger than the oldest student in the class, which was stressful for him. I discovered that in Sweden, girls start kindergarten at age five, one year ahead of boys, because there seems to be significant developmental differences between boys and girls in school achievement in the early grades. Eventually Ralph achieved academic success both in high school and college, majoring on physics and applied math. He became a computer software engineer and excels in his field. He and his wife, Joni, have a lovely daughter, Raizel, who is applying to medical school. Joel also did extremely well in school, studying physics and computer science. Joel and his wife, Glenda, have two children, Langley and Tenaya, both of whom are doing well in college.

Job at The UC Berkeley Donner Laboratory

After placing the boys in their schools, I concentrated on trying to find a job on the UC campus. My strategy was to attend seminars and audit classes to meet some professors. This proved successful. I met Dr. David Freifelder at a biochemistry lecture. He was a physical biochemist who was a professor at the Donner Lab at UC Berkeley. Dr. Freifelder was searching for a bacteriologist/geneticist who could work on mutations, specifically radiation damage to bacterial and viral DNA. I fit the job description and he hired me immediately. I was fortunate to be able to join his research group, and found it extremely intellectually stimulating. The group was dynamic, and I enjoyed working there immensely. David Freifelder and I published several papers together, and I became good friends with David and his wife, Dr. Dorothy Freifelder. In later years Ralph worked as a summer intern in the Freifelder's lab at Brandeis in Massachusetts.

David and I found some interesting genetic variants in bacterial antibiotic resistance strains. Some strains of *E.coli* were extremely sensitive to radiation while others were quite resistant. I monitored the background radiation in our lab, to be able to measure the increase in sensitivity to radiation in our strains. To my astonishment, there were several days with an unusually high background radiation. I remarked on this to Hugh who said that they correlated with atmospheric nuclear tests in Nevada, which were later found to have seriously affected the health of US Veterans in the Nevada desert. The dates and intensity of the nuclear tests in Nevada were not reported at the time and many of the soldiers who were present in a simulated battlefield situation developed cancers and other radiation-induced problems. Hugh became very involved with helping the widows of the soldier get recognition and compensation for the death of their husbands.

Dr. David Freifelder was eventually recruited to head the Biochemistry department at Brandeis University. His group at Berkeley was dissolved, and my job ended. I was pregnant with our third child at that time, so I decided to take some time off from work and be a stay-at-home-mom. This worked well because Hugh was invited to lecture at the University in Mexico City for a summer semester and later for a year at the University of Iowa in Iowa City, so I would have had to give up my job in order to accompany him. It was always clear that Hugh's professional career was primary and more important and successful than mine, and that he would achieve brilliantly in physics. I loved my scientific career but had no illusions about my productivity, while I was dividing my time and energy between being a mom and a scientist.

Birth of Our Daughter, Laila

Our third child, Laila Ruth, was born on January 4, 1967 at Alta Bates Hospital where our two boys were also born. I shared a labor room with a very good friend from Europe, Enike Schram, who had come to Berkeley from Holland with her physicist husband and their five children for a sabbatical year. The Schrams stayed in our house while they were house-hunting, during the time that Hugh and I were away on a short spring vacation. Both Enike and I became pregnant around the same time, and we joked that we might have our babies on the same day. I reluctantly gave Enike the name of my obstetrician, and we laughed at the thought that he might have to deliver both babies at the same time, and that is exactly what happened. I entered the labor room and there was Enike, in an advanced stage of labor, having serious difficulties and drawing the attention of the entire staff. Laila was in breech position, and I was scheduled for a C-section, that was delayed for many hours because of staffing problem. The staff was engaged with Enike's birth problems, as she had a huge uterine tumor that was obstructing her delivery. By the time 30 hours had elapsed, it was too late to do a C-section as Laila's little butt had already emerged. It was a traumatic day, because Enike's baby passed away, during surgery for heart abnormalities.

The nurses told me that Laila was the most beautiful baby they had ever seen. Of course, being unbiased, I agreed that Laila was absolutely stunningly beautiful. I had conflicted feelings, though, as my good friend had just lost her baby boy, Alexander, and I didn't feel comfortable being in the same room where Enike was grieving and seeing priests and medical specialists. It was a painful and sad situation. Enike and I bonded strongly after her loss, and she doted on Laila. The Schrams adopted a baby girl about one year afterwards, while they were living in Rochester, New York, before returning to Holland. Laila was a very sweet and easy baby who smiled and gurgled with happiness. Ralph and Joel played with their little sister, and Ralph even babysat for Laila even though he was only seven years old. I had a wonderful little family and I was extremely happy, although I missed my scientific career.

My Mother's Cancer, 1967

Laila was an adorable and easy baby, and I really enjoyed being at home and not working during her infancy. I worried about being able to return to work after losing professional time in a fast-moving field. During this period, I was facing tragedy as well. My mother, who lived on the East Coast in Middletown, NY, had been diagnosed with stage four colorectal cancer, so I needed to fly to the East Coast frequently to visit her with my nursing baby, while Hugh stayed with the boys. The first flight to visit my mother was in late May, 1967, when she had her first surgery. She was in a deep depression, lying in bed and facing the wall, and I had to comfort both her and my father. I spent my time visiting my mother in the hospital, nursing Laila and comforting my father. I arranged for a housekeeper who would take care of my mother when she was able to leave the hospital. By the time I returned to Berkeley on June 10, 1967, I found out that I had completely missed the Israeli Six-Day War during which Israel recaptured Jerusalem, the heart and soul of the Jewish people. I had been so deeply absorbed by my mother's illness that I missed the important event.

My father made me swear that I would never tell my mother

her true diagnosis. I had to pretend to accept the fictional diagnosis that Dad invented. It was a very difficult situation, since my mother was very smart and saw through the deception. I reassured her that she would get well again, but she had a very hard time with the surgery and chemotherapy (which we called vitamin supplements) and with her colostomy that embarrassed her. She was convinced that she would die, and I couldn't give her the comfort of being honest and helping her express her wishes and fears.

It was difficult to enjoy my gorgeous baby while worrying about my mother. After much suffering, she died just a few months after her surgery. I dreaded leaving my father alone in his apartment in Middletown, but my father insisted on staying close to where my mother was buried and where he was still employed as a geriatric psychiatrist. He wanted to visit her grave frequently. He could not let her go.

Chicken Pox

Hugh took the boys camping during one of my visits to my mother during her illness. He invited two of their friends, and they had a wonderful time except that one of the friends was incubating chicken pox. Our boys caught chicken pox virus and Joel also developed a blistering Poison Oak dermatitis, contracted while peeing in the bushes. By the time I returned from visiting my mother, Joel was in agony as he had chicken pox in addition to the poison oak rash. He really suffered during this time. Ralph's chicken pox case was somewhat milder and Laila, who was still nursing, had only a mild case because she was still nursing and receiving my protective antibodies. She had contracted the infection from her brothers after our return.

Sanne and Joel (sitting next to me), Laila (next to
Joel) and Ralph in foreground, about 1969

Anti-War Demonstrations in Berkeley
(1969)

The war in Vietnam was escalating, and the students on the Berkeley campus were deeply involved with anti-war demonstrations, rallies, teach-ins and sit-ins in UC's Sproul Plaza. Crowds protested the arrest of campus students on Sproul Plaza by the UC Police Department. Students took over campus buildings, including the administration building. This was the era of the My Lei Massacre and the invasion of Cambodia.

The UC students and faculty were horrified by the US military actions in Vietnam. There were daily demonstrations that expanded from the campus into the city. One day when I was in downtown, with Laila in my baby backpack, I heard helicopters hovering over campus, and we were soon enveloped in tear gas. I needed to get out of the area in a hurry because Laila and I were both choking. The California Highway Patrol, The Berkeley Police and the National Guard Troops were on the streets, and the atmosphere was very tense.

The police arrested some demonstrators and many were sent to the Santa Rita Jail. This was the era of "Free Speech" rallies, sit-ins and demonstrations against the Vietnam War. The National Guard was present in the streets of Berkeley, and helicopters flew overhead. Violence against the demonstrators by the police and National Guard led to the "People's Park" event, during which at least one person, James Rector, was killed, on "Bloody Thursday" May 15, 1969. Alan Blanchard was blinded, and the police inflicted injuries on the protesters. Several other demonstrators were injured on Telegraph Avenue. I was horrified by the bombings and atrocities of the war and the My Lai Massacre in 1969, and I was shocked by the violence against the anti-war protesters.

Governor Reagan was publicly critical of university administrators for tolerating student demonstrations at the Berkeley campus. He had received popular support during his 1966 gubernatorial campaign for promising to crack down on what the public perceived as a generally lax attitude at California's public universities. Reagan called the Berkeley campus "a haven for communist sympathizers, protesters, and sex deviants." Reagan considered the creation of Peoples' Park a direct leftist challenge to the property rights of the university, and this emboldened the university to crack down on the students. Reagan sent the California Highway Patrol to control the anti-war protesters.

Mexico City (1969)

In 1969 Hugh received an invitation to teach at the National Autonomous University of Mexico City, that had a huge student body of over three hundred thousand students. We spent two wonderful months during the summer of 1970. It was a relief to get away from Berkeley and recover from my mother's death, my job loss, various illnesses and the demonstrations. Hugh's summer position as a visiting professor was very nice for him, but I had to entertain the three kids in an apartment in the Pink Zone (*Zona Roza*) of Mexico City. The kids and I made numerous visits to the spectacular anthropology museum in Chapultapec park, and the boys learned so much that they could have led tours.

I made plenty of mistakes while I was trying to keep house in Mexico City because I did not speak Spanish. I once took a load of dirty diapers to what I thought was a laundromat, "*lavar.*" I didn't realize that it was actually a dry cleaner, "*secadora.*" The diapers were dry-cleaned, which cost a fortune, and I soon learned Spanish for laundromat from Spanish speaking friends. A more serious mistake occurred when I gave all three kids baths, not realizing that the gas water heater was not vented properly, and I had not left a window open. Laila was the first to lose consciousness, followed by Joel and then Ralph feeling sick. I had a severe headache went to a neighbor who called an ambulance. All of us had carbon monoxide poisoning from which we recovered in fresh air, but it was a big scare and we decided to move out of the apartment with its faulty ventilation.

Our Move to a House in The Pedregal

One of Hugh's former physics graduate students, Professor Fernando del Rio, was his host at the university. Fernando arranged our move into the house of a professor who was on a sabbatical in Berkeley. The family had a lovely home in the fancy Pedregal district and had live-in servants. When we moved to the house, we discovered that the live-in couple had a lovely little daughter who was the same age as Laila. The two little girls became friends, and Laila started to learn how to speak Spanish. The house had many bedrooms, so I invited my teenaged cousin, Beatrice, from Chicago, and my father to spend some weeks with us in our luxury house. Beatrice, who was a very beautiful 16-year-old, attracted lots of attention when we went to the university campus. We were trailed by some students who wanted to practice speaking English with us. We made friends with the students, and they became wonderful tour guides in the city.

Hugh drove our VW minibus daily to the University to give lectures, and he enjoyed having our landlord's "servant," Gabriel, open the gate of the house to let in our "Hippy" bus. The house owners had probably driven a fancy car, and these crazy Americanos drove an old and dirty minibus, which embarrassed Gabriel. He finally couldn't stand it anymore, and he washed our bus to spare himself the embarrassment of opening the gate for our vehicle, which in his opinion, was below our status.

Visits from My Family and Students as Tour Guides

My cousin Beatrice and my father joined us for daily local trips in and around Mexico City. They enjoyed the gorgeous house that we had rented and the many interesting sights. Beatrice continued to be a big hit with the students on campus. We drove to campus almost every day, and we always quickly ended up with a group of students following us. One of the students was in a medical program and he invited my father to one of his anatomy classes. My father was delighted with the tour of the medical school. He particularly enjoyed the section with the corpses were used in the anatomy class. It was difficult to drag my Dad away from the classroom and the corpses. The students also toured us around and accompanied our little family on a tour of the pyramids in Tenochtitlan, northeast of Mexico City, where the boys had a fantastic time climbing up the steep pyramids and afterwards eating in local restaurants.

One restaurant featured eel pizza and Joel, an adventurous 8-year-old, was eager to order this exotic item. I told him that he could order the eel pizza but that he would have to eat it. When it arrived, the little tiny pairs of eyes of the baby eels looked too disgusting to eat, but Joel bravely started to devour the pizza. After a while he started to turn green and vomited on the table. I don't blame him—the pizza really looked horrible. Joel claims that he vomited because he over-ate.

Moon Landing, Mexican Vacation in Acapulco

After Beatrice and my father left, we sent Ralph and Joel to a Mexican summer camp where they could swim and do sports while Hugh and I, along with Laila, took a short vacation. We drove through the lovely countryside and visited small towns. We stayed at tourist hotels and ate delicious meals. One fantastic trip was to Acapulco, where—on July 20, 1969—we watched TV with the locals and saw Neal Armstrong and Buzz Aldrin plant the American flag on the Moon. What an incredible sight in such a beautiful place! All of the viewers applauded and drank to the lunar landing. It was a thrilling moment to share with the Mexicans. I wish that we could have stayed in Mexico longer, but we needed to get back to Berkeley so the boys could go back to school and Hugh could get back to work at the lab.

Back to Berkeley and Various Panics

As soon as we returned to Berkeley, school was the priority. Due to the implementation of "racial integration" in the Berkeley school system, the boys attended two different schools. Schools that served first through sixth grades were divided into two groups: first through third grades, and fourth through sixth grades. Bussing would compensate for clustering of racial groups in separate geographical areas. Ralph went to "big" Hillside school and Joel to "little" Hillside so it was impossible to attend both PTA meetings that were always planned on the same night.

One Friday afternoon Ralph did not arrive home from school. I became very anxious and called all of his friends, but he was nowhere to be found. Late in the afternoon I received a phone call from the principal of his school saying that Ralph was still in the school building and that I should come and pick him up. He had been found by a janitor in the attic of the school, where he had been sent by the teacher for a minor classroom misconduct. When the school day ended, the teacher forgot him and dismissed the other students, who went home in the school bus. I was shocked at the negligence of the teacher, that might have resulted in Ralph's being locked in the school for the weekend. I should have sued the school, but my relief was so great that I never considered it.

I had another near panic when one day a friend of Joel's came to our house and said that Joel had fallen into the shaft of a missile silo on the Nike Missile Trail in Tilden Regional Park. The old missile site had been abandoned long before, but the site had not been labeled, closed or covered. I took a friend and we hiked about a mile on the Nimitz Trail and found Joel, who had been unable to climb out of the launch shaft. Joel would have disappeared forever if his friend hadn't alerted me. I never recovered from those frights.

I became active in the PTA of both the boy's schools. I served on the principal selection committee for Longfellow School. Ralph's school was one of the "feeder" schools for Longfellow, so I attended meetings in order to read the resumes of the applicants. I faced a huge pile of applications, but was told that I needn't read most of them because it was already decided that the Longfellow PTA wanted only a black male principal. When I asked if these specifications were included in the advertisement for the position, I was told that they were not included because that would be illegal. My reply was that if it were illegal, then I needed to review all of the applications. I was then ordered to leave the meeting immediately or else be subject to a citizen's arrest. I resigned in protest. In the future I would participate only in bake sales and other fund-raising activities for the PTA. I am disappointed that no coalition developed between the Black and the Jewish communities to fight racism and anti-Semitism.

My Attempt to Turn to the Arts

I spent some of my time taking piano lessons and taking lessons in a pottery workshop. These were very rewarding hobbies, but I realized that I wasn't gifted in the arts even though I enjoyed them. I still have some of the pottery items I made, and I am horrified by how bad they are. I also took guitar lessons, but I was hopeless. The neck on the beautiful guitar, which I had bought in Mexico, was too large for my small hands. I longed to get back into the lab and do genetics research, but it would be several more years until I was able to reenter my field and find employment. I was terribly frustrated and concerned by my lack of professional work and lack of income, and I worried about being able to re-enter my profession.

Hugh's Disaffection with Livermore (1972)

Iowa City

Hugh had been working at the Lawrence Livermore Laboratory for about 15 years and had become disillusioned. He felt sick about the direction the lab had taken under the directorship of Dr. Edward Teller. When Hugh joined the lab in 1957 he was a member of the Theoretical Division, which allowed him to do research in his field of statistical mechanics and properties of dense plasmas. The lab no longer wanted to support a theoretical physics division but wanted the scientists to work on thermonuclear weapons development. Hugh resisted taking on any classified assignments and wanted to focus on theoretical, not weapons, research. He ached to get an appointment in an academic institution and was lucky to receive an offer at the University of Iowa, in Iowa City, as a visiting professor. Our physicist friend, Dr. David Montgomery, engineered the appointment and assured Hugh that it might lead to a permanent academic position. In August of 1972, we drove our VW minibus across the country to Iowa City and settled into a nice rental home near the city park. Our dog, Machi, a male Golden Retriever, jumped out of the car and ran into the park which had a beautiful municipal swimming pool. Machi jumped into the water and the next morning we saw his picture on the front page of the local Iowa paper. That was the beginning of our wonderful year in Iowa – a big relief after chaotic Berkeley.

Iowa City, Friendly and Welcoming

I arrived in Iowa City with a deep prejudice that everyone living in the Midwest was a conservative bigot, but I quickly changed my mind. The Iowans were warm, hospitable, generous and welcoming. Our neighbors were friendly as were the members of the physics department and the Jewish community. We had so many invitations during the first two weeks that I hardly prepared any dinners at home. The teachers welcomed the boys and were very kind, and they made sure that their classmates included them in games and home invitations.

The Jewish community was socially and politically active, and the Rabbi, Rabbi Diamond, and the congregants helped our family feel at home. There were weekly Sunday brunches and we became close friends with many very interesting people. Several of the families, including the Rabbi, were ardent Zionists and were planning to make *Aliya* (immigration to Israel). That rekindled my strong desire to immigrate to Israel. I met with a *Shaliach* (recruiter for Israel) to see what I needed to do to prepare to make such a move. I attended an elementary Hebrew course and met with the families who were preparing to move to Israel. Unfortunately, Hugh did not support my plan. He wasn't brought up in a Zionist atmosphere, and professional opportunities in Israel seemed scarce. Hugh was prepared to make professional visits to Israeli universities and institutes, but he was not in favor of a permanent move. This was very disappointing to me, but I could certainly understand his objection to relocating his professional life.

I spent much of my time taking pottery classes and auditing genetics courses at the university. I returned home by the time that the kids were finished with school each day. I made many friends and enjoyed my Iowa visit. Ralph and Joel enjoyed their schools and made friends. They went to Hebrew School and enjoyed sports, especially bicycle riding and skating.

Laila went to a very "alternative" nursery school, which was staffed with longhaired young men and earthy, hairy-legged young women. The atmosphere was child friendly and relaxed with a program of singing, dancing, planting vegetable gardens, cooking and story-telling. The children seemed very happy in this loose atmosphere, and Laila made friends with the other children. The parents were very supportive of self-expression and creativity and were not obsessed with preparing the children for academics. The kids learned a great deal from their activities—probably more than if they had been sitting at desks and working at pre-reading. Laila suffered from lots of colds and earaches and went through a period of hearing loss. The hearing loss made her irritable in school because she couldn't hear directions from the teachers and missed out on some of her favorite activities. It also made her screech when she talked.

The University of Iowa medical school had a superb pediatric department, and Laila was diagnosed with hearing loss and chronic inflammation of the inner ear. The recommendation was to insert ear tubes, a minor surgical intervention. The procedure was successful and improved the hearing, but swimming was prohibited. This became a problem in the hot summer months when Laila was aching to go swimming along with her brothers, but she was a real trouper and accepted the situation. Eventually, the ear tubes disappeared, but she needed a tonsillectomy to prevent any more ear and throat infections.

One of the best things about our stay in Iowa City was that Hugh was able to bicycle to the physics department, but the worst thing was the intense heat of summer and the freezing cold of winter. I worried constantly that, when he bicycled home, he would skid off the road and wind up in the freezing Iowa River. One evening, Hugh was preparing to give an important seminar and decided to return to his office after dinner to do some more preparation. While he was gone I baked a cake to welcome him home, hoping to spend a relaxing evening, but he didn't return as expected. I waited until 5:00 AM and became extremely worried because I was convinced that he had skidded into the freezing river. I called his office and there was no answer, so I expected the worst. When he finally arrived at home, close to 6:00 AM, he explained that he had found an error in one of his calculations and he spent several hours in the library looking up scientific papers in order to correct his error. I was relieved to have him back at home but furious that he hadn't called. His explanation was that he had lost track of time and didn't call because he did not want to wake me up. I explained that I hadn't slept at all and that I had been very concerned. That was the bachelor in him.

Machi, our Golden Retriever, loved the Iowa River, and one day he swam from Iowa City to Cedar Rapids, a distance of 60 miles. He was fished out of the river by fraternity students, who called us and told us that Machi was sitting on their couch watching TV with them while they were drinking beer, and they asked us if we would come and get him. They wanted to keep him, but he was happy to come home with us.

Machi got into lots of trouble in Iowa City. One time he swallowed a needle that I only knew because there was a thread hanging out of his mouth. I had to rush him in for emergency surgery. Another serious event happened in early Spring. Machi chased migrating ducks resting on a frozen pond, and fell through the ice. I called and tried to tempt him to come out with treats and bones, but I was unable to get him to come back onto land. When Hugh came home from work in the evening, he had to wade into the water and drag Machi out. The dog had been in the water for six hours and was completely water logged. He actually sloshed when Hugh walked him home, and he peed for about 20 minutes. Snot was flowing out of his nose and I was convinced he had pneumonia, so I gave him some antibiotics, which had just been prescribed for Joel's "strep" throat, and wrapped him in blankets. I took Machi to the vet the next morning, and he said that I probably saved his life by giving him the antibiotics. I then called the pediatrician to get more antibiotics so that Joel could finish his course of treatment.

We led a very active social life in Iowa City facilitated by our good friends, David and Shirley Montgomery, who had lived in Iowa City for several years and knew everybody in the physics department. The locals loved to throw brunch and dinner parties, so we had plenty of great food to eat and stimulating conversations. One of the topics was the Vietnam War, which everybody opposed. I was surprised to find out how much drinking occurred in Iowa compared to Berkeley. Berkeley was obsessed with marijuana, and I dreaded going to social events where everyone was giggling at some joke that I never understood. I was never able to drink much, as I became extremely nauseous after even a moderate amount of alcohol. Apparently, I don't make enough alcohol dehydrogenase to detoxify my drinks. Hugh was able to manage and enjoy it, to my surprise.

Music Lessons

Our house was directly across the street from the new University of Iowa Music department, so we were able to go to many free concerts. The bonus was that we found excellent piano and clarinet teachers for Ralph and Joel. Joel's clarinet teacher, who was married to a pianist, once baked a bread "flute" with a recorder inside and, after playing the concert, he ate the bread flute. The audience was delighted, and Joel was thrilled. Ralph's piano teacher was also excellent.

Visit from Hugh's Mother

Hugh's mother, Verna, loved to drive. One day she surprised us, appearing with no prior announcement. It was a wonderful and totally unexpected surprise. One of the first things that Verna did was to open her large handbag and let out three tiny baby chicks, which she had brought all the way from Palo Alto. The chicks were delighted to get out of the bag and run around the house, but we had to make sure that Machi couldn't get anywhere near them. He would have certainly eaten them. Verna visited us for a few days and then took her chicks and drove to her farm in Arkansas. My Dad also visited us from his home in Middletown, but he didn't bring any chickens. He loved visiting the Iowa City medical school and made friends with the doctors at our Jewish community. He seemed very sad without my mother, so Hugh and I plotted to get him to move to Berkeley so he could be close to our family. He loved his grand-children and they cheered him up immensely.

Chicago

We managed to take a short trip to Chicago to visit my Uncle and Aunt, Ernst and Marlise. They showed us around Chicago's museums, parks, theaters and Lake Michigan. It was difficult to keep Machi from jumping into the lake. We had to keep him on two short leashes, and it took two people to keep him from dashing into the water.

We also visited good old friends from Berkeley, professors Sylvia and Ved Vatuk, and their four children in their apartment in Chicago. Ved was a folklorist and Sylvia was an anthropologist. They entertained us with lots of good stories and songs. In the morning, our boys went outside to where our minibus was parked and came back telling us that our bus had been stolen. We thought that they were playing a trick on us so were shocked to find out that it really was gone. We called the manager of the apartment house who told us that it had been towed because the manager did not realize that we were the Vatuk's guests and were using their designated parking space. It took the rest of the day and a lot of money for the towing, to retrieve it, but we finally got it back.

After our trip to Chicago we drove to Arkansas to visit

Hugh's mother's farm. We all had a grand time reconnecting with Hugh's sister's family who were living next door to Grandma Verna's home. Neva and her husband had five lively children, and the cousins enjoyed playing in the barn and in the pasture as well as setting off Estes model rockets that Hugh and the boys built. We visited the old school where Verna had taught and the nearby city of Monticello. Monticello is a charming old-fashioned Southern town about seven miles from the Hughes-DeWitt farm. Many of Grandma Verna's extended family lived nearby, and we had a chance to meet the hospitable Arkansas folks. Monticello is home to the University of Arkansas' "Boll Weevils & Cotton Blossoms" and the university's culture was very different from Berkeley's ultra-liberal atmosphere. It was a real education in Southern hospitality and politics.

Job Hunting for Hugh

It seemed increasingly unlikely that Iowa was going to offer Hugh an academic position because the university had declared a hiring moratorium, so he gave a series of seminars at a number of other universities, hoping for an offer. I dreaded the times when Hugh was away giving lectures during the icy winter because, invariably, things went wrong at home. During one of his trips away, there was a huge snowstorm. The icy wind blew out the pilot light in the heating system. The house temperature dropped, the phone lines were down, and our driveway was piled up with snow. I was stuck in the cold house with the kids, and we huddled together with our golden retriever for warmth. The house remained freezing cold, until I was able to get the local heating company to come and turn the heater back on. I was spoiled by California's mild weather, and I had to learn to cope with Iowa's fierce weather.

One freezing night when I was home alone with the kids, Joel stepped on a big darning needle. It went in so deeply that I couldn't pull it out. I needed to take him to the emergency room, but the driveway was piled high with snow. After an hour of shoveling, with Joel crying in pain, I managed to pull our car out of the driveway and drive him to the local hospital, leaving Ralph to baby sit for Laila. We were lucky to get immediate attention. The attending physician gave Joel a local anesthetic and was able to pull out the needle.

Massacre at Kent State University

Anti-Vietnam War protests were being held at many universities. In May of 1970, there was a dreadful shooting at Kent State University in Ohio. Four unarmed students protesting the invasion of Cambodia were shot and killed by the National Guard, and nine other students were wounded. In Jackson State College in Mississippi students were shot at on May 15th, with two deaths and twelve injuries. There was a significant national response, and many schools were closed as a result of a strike by four million students. Students at the University of Iowa were outraged and held protests. The state legislature responded by cutting the University funding, which resulted in a hiring freeze, and Hugh could not be offered a position on the faculty.

Hugh went on many job-hunting trips, but no offers were made. It was clear that he was not going to receive a faculty position at the University of Iowa, so Hugh resigned himself to returning to Livermore after his sabbatical year. This was a huge professional disappointment, although we were happy to return to our house and rejoin our Berkeley friends and community.

Our Trip West Across the Country

At the end of the academic year in Iowa, Hugh decided to make two cross-country trips. First he drove our VW bug, which full of the pottery I had made, back to Berkeley. Then he flew back to Iowa City to pick up our family and Machi and make the drive a second time in our minibus. We said good-bye to our Iowa friends, crammed into our VW minibus, and set off for the West Coast. Within 50 miles, Machi vomited all over the back. We had to stop and clean everything up, losing a travel day. Poor Machi. He had eaten too many of the bones that we had distracted him with while packing up the van. After we cleaned up, we drove north to Minneapolis, Minnesota, where we had good friends from Hugh's Stanford and Los Alamos days—Dr. Harry Foreman and his wife, Billie, who was a contemporary of Hugh's at Stanford. The Formans were gracious hosts, and we stayed a few days in order to get reacquainted and see the local sights.

We left Minneapolis and drove west over the Mississippi, where Machi decided take a swim. He refused to come out of the water, and we managed to lose another day because of his behavior. When he finally got out of the river, we had to run him until his fur was dry so he wouldn't smell up the car. The trip across the U.S. was very beautiful. We stopped at many exciting places such as Yellowstone National Park and other national monuments. Our kids were fascinated by the dinosaur fossils at the Badlands National Park in South Dakota. The fossils were beautifully preserved, and many were still *in situ* from 75 to 67 million years ago.

The high point of our trip was camping in Yellowstone in Wyoming. "Old Faithful" performed for us, and we saw the canyons, geysers, wild animals, and beautiful rivers in this wonderful park. The trails around the geysers had wooden footpaths, which Joel navigated barefoot. He got a huge splinter in the bottom of his foot, which dug deeply into his flesh. We went to an emergency station to get it extracted. Later, the wound got infected and Joel limped for several weeks after the accident.

We usually camped at night, but we ate combinations of breakfast and lunch at cafes on the highway. One morning, after eating heartily, we got into our mini-bus and continued on our way west. After about half an hour Laila asked, "where is Joel?" We looked around and realized that Joel was not in the car, so we turned around and drove back to our breakfast stop. Poor Joel, who was just nine years old, was standing there outside the cafe looking forlorn and very sad. He had gotten out of the mini-bus after we were fully loaded to make a quick bathroom stop. We hadn't noticed that we'd driven off, missing one of our kids!

Camping in Colorado

We eventually reached Montana, where a good friend from Hugh's days at Stanford, Dr. Bea Vogel, lived near a lake with her two young children. Bea was an expert on high altitude spiders and butterflies, and she had amazing stories to tell about her collection. Bea's boat was in dry dock, and Hugh helped her launch the boat into the lake for the summer season. He spent a great deal of time in the water launching the boat, but he was hypothermic when he got back onto dry land. The next day he developed a fever and was completely exhausted and seemed to be suffering from flu. Hugh was very stoic and continued to drive us on to Monument National Park where Machi got loose once again. It took hours to find him and get him back. It was a stressful and difficult day. After a night's worth of camping, we continued on a northwest route.

Mount Rainier in the Cascades, Washington

Hugh had camped and climbed on Mount Rainier when he was a student at Stanford, and he wanted to show the kids an active volcano, so we detoured to Mt. Rainier. We had a spectacular view of this magnificent mountain, and I am happy that one of our grandchildren, Langley, who is attending the University of Washington, goes skiing there. Mount Rainier is close to Seattle where my cousin, Eva, lived with her family. We continued our way homeward, driving south along the scenic coast, past the redwoods and the volcanoes—Shasta and Lassen. Everyone who visits the U.S. should see these world wonders. After leaving Seattle, Hugh developed severe numbness in his fingers and toes and was unable to feel the pedals on the car. He couldn't even hold a spoon or fork. We stopped in Portland, Oregon, where I took him to a hospital, and they diagnosed Guillain-Barre syndrome (GBS), a neurological disorder that attacks the peripheral nervous system. There was no treatment for the syndrome, which was probably the result of the flu-like illness that Hugh had gotten at the icy lake in Montana. I drove the rest of the way to Berkeley. Fortunately, by the time we arrived home, Hugh had recovered some feeling in his feet.

Fantastic Country

The trip across the northern part of the USA was absolutely fantastic, even though we had some problems along the way. I was impressed with the beauty and diversity of the land. The plants and animals were absolutely stupendous, and I thoroughly appreciated and loved the national parks. The trip made environmentalists out of all of us. We are now dedicated to preserving the grandeur of the landscape. The Rockies, Tetons, Cascades, and Sierras—the wild rivers and deserts are a wonder. I am so grateful I have experienced all of this diversity and beauty.

Return to The East Bay

Our tenants, the Arber family, had a lease on our house until September, so we drove to Hugh's mother's house in Palo Alto to stay until their lease expired. Dr. Werner Arber, a Swiss microbiologist and geneticist, wrote a seminal article on gene transduction by bacteriophage P1, the very 'phage I had used to transduce the male sexuality gene in *E. coli*. It was fun to be able to rent our house to the scientist who enabled me to do my graduate work at UCB. Dr. Arber was a co-recipient of the Nobel Prize in physiology or medicine in 1978.

Grandma Verna lived near the Stanford campus. She owned a half-acre of apricot trees and had a nursery school on her property. The boys had a terrific time sleeping in a tent in the apricot orchard, and they picked apricots for sale. They each earned enough to pay for half the price of a three-speed bike, which we helped pay for with matching grants. Laila attended the Ruth Woods Nursery located on the DeWitt property. There was a swimming pool near the orchard, so we could all cool off in the afternoons, except for Laila who still had ear tubes. The kids had a wonderful month living at Grandma's home, while Hugh commuted to Livermore.

After a few weeks we moved back to the East Bay (Kensington), to the house of our dear friends, the Lehmans, who were temporarily away from Berkeley. Dr. Sherman Lehman was a professor of mathematics at Berkeley who had studied at Stanford at the same time as Hugh. Sherman was brilliant and eccentric and had lived in a tent on the Stanford campus while he was a student, together with the younger son of the aviator Charles Lindbergh (Lindbergh's baby was kidnapped for ransom in 1932). Sherman and his wife, Lilian, were fellow rock climbers at Stanford, and they were happy to let us stay in their house while they were away with their five children.

Photos of My Young Family – Ralph, Joel and Laila
(circa 1969)

Back in Our Berkeley House

We settled back home in Berkeley shortly before school began. Our tenants, the Arbers, were a lovely Swiss family, and had kept the house in beautiful shape, but they had not used the finished basement. I had left a 30-pound bag of dog food in the laundry area, and rodents had converted it into 30 pounds of mouse feces. I had a big job cleaning up the disaster, and I developed bronchitis from the dust of rodent debris. It was horrible. Next time I needed to clean a dirty area, I am resolved to wear a particle mask. Coincidentally, it was Werner Arber who had discovered that P1 bacteriophage could be used to transfer genes from one bacterium to another – a tool that I used extensively in my graduate research project. The Arbers took great care of our cat, so much so that she delivered three kittens the day we arrived home as a homecoming gift.

School

The boys returned to the Berkeley public schools, which were a disappointment compared to the great Iowa schools they had attended the previous year. Ralph was in 6th grade in Iowa when I heard of a new experimental public school named Odyssey, later nicknamed "Idiocy," which at the time, sounded fantastic. Ralph applied, and was accepted to the 7th grade. Odyssey was located in the Lawrence Hall of Science, walking distance from our house. The school emphasized science and giving students free range of the facilities at the LHS museum. Unfortunately, the school director was totally incompetent and had not bothered to renew the contract with LHS, so the school moved to temporary quarters in trailers near another Berkeley school. The staff was completely discouraged and left, so there was no longer a trace of the old science curriculum or the special facilities at LHS. The new director was also incompetent and had not signed the necessary insurance documents, so the school could not function at the new location. The rest of the year was spent in recruiting new staff and finding a location for the school.

A new director was found who had a poor attitude about achieving "racial" integration, and wound up splintering the student body. Each student was expected to start a project that would include other students. Ralph decided to start a chess club as he was an avid player and was already tutoring a group of kids after school. The director told him that chess was a "Whitey's game" and would not authorize the project. I tried to argue with him, because I knew that black students were good chess players at the local YMCA chess club, but it didn't help. Another project Ralph wanted to start was building a Zuck-erman harpsichord. He had saved his Bar Mitzvah money and, together with a matching grant from us, bought a Zuckerman harpsichord kit, which Hugh helped him build. The director had the same objection to the harpsichord carpentry project, which he also called a "Whitey project." This was very discouraging because the director was clearly promoting offensive cultural stereotypes. At the end of the school year, the director "borrowed" the school's musical instruments for his own private music school. He was eventually fired, and the school subsequently collapsed. The original idea was fantastic, a science school at the Hall of Science, but it was destroyed because of staff infighting and incompetence. In summary, Ralph's 7th grade school year was a disaster.

Hugh went to the superintendent, complained loudly, and we finally got a transfer for Ralph, back into the regular school system. The school system was so disorganized that Ralph was placed into the 9th grade, which caused him to skip the 8th grade entirely. This was an excellent outcome, and Ralph was pleased to be placed at that grade level.

Ralph took piano lessons and was making very good progress, but his teacher was extremely eccentric and unstable. I also took lessons from her and I found her to be temperamental, narcissistic and erratic. Fortunately, she eventually moved away, and we found a very gifted young pianist who took over the piano lessons.

Joel had a great year and thrived in his 6th grade class. He had a good teachers and many friends. Joel was lively and loved skateboarding and his clarinet lessons. Both boys attended Hebrew School two afternoons a week and on Sunday mornings, so they had very busy schedules.

Laila spent one more year in pre-school, the New School, before entering first grade in our local public school. She was surprised and disappointed that she didn't learn to read on her very first day of first grade. She was passionately interested in ballet and enrolled in a ballet school in Berkeley, where she immediately showed talent. Ballet became a very large part of her life and she went to five classes per week. She made great friends in her ballet class and seemed to be a very happy and energetic kid. One endearing quality that Laila had was kindness. Whenever she had a party or invited kids over to play, she insisted on inviting kids who were shy or were left out of school social functions. She had empathy for "underdog" kids and had a great sense of compassion. Laila was artistic and was proficient in calligraphy and drawing. I was delighted, because I had no talent in those skills.

Jewish Life

Before our year in Iowa, Hugh and I had led a secular life, except for celebrating the Jewish holidays. But once the boys started Hebrew School in Iowa City, we became addicted to the bagel and lox Sunday brunches at the synagogue. The Rabbi was intelligent and interesting, and the congregation was welcoming. We decided to join the congregation and became involved with the Iowa City Jewish Community—a very rewarding association. My passion for Zionism was renewed so I contacted the *Shaliach* (Israeli emissary) to investigate making *Aliya* (moving to Israel). Although Hugh was not keen on making the move, I was determined to visit Israel frequently and to send the kids on Israel programs.

My mother had been an ardent Zionist since her youth and had planned on immigrating to Palestine, as it was then called. She belonged to an association called *"BlauWeiss,"* meaning "Blue White," which prepared young people for the move to Palestine. Her plans were thwarted because she had so many obligations in Germany. Her disabled brother needed help and her sister, Thekla, had a serious heart condition caused by having scarlet fever as a child. Her sister died, leaving three young children, my cousins Max, Hannah and Eva. My mother helped her sister, Thekla, during her illness and then briefly cared for the children after Thekla died. It was impossible for my mother to immigrate to Palestine (now Israel), but she never let go of that dream. She joined Hadassah, a women's association started by an admirable woman named Henrietta Szold, who was dedicated to providing medical care for Jews in Palestine, and who gave money and time and education to support public health. I became a life member of Hadassah and gave life-memberships to Hadassah to all of my children and grandchildren.

On our return to Berkeley we decided to join a local Synagogue, Congregation Beth El, which had an afternoon Hebrew School and a very liberal congregation. It was time to start preparing Ralph and Joel for their Bar Mitzvah training, and we needed the support of the Jewish community for those events. There were two synagogues that we knew of in Berkeley at that time, Beth El, a Reform congregation, and Beth Israel, an Orthodox congregation. I felt that Beth El would be more comfortable for Hugh, who lacked a Jewish background. So we sent the kids to Beth El Hebrew School. Most of their friends went to Beth El, so it seemed natural and comfortable for our family. We still have many friends whom we made during that time in our lives.

I was shocked at how Berkley and the whole Bay Area had been transformed while we were away. The annual folk music festival was now devoted to ear-splittingly loud rock music with unintelligible screeching and screaming. The women all had hairy legs and body piercings, and wore no bras. The guys all had long stringy (dirty) hair and beards. Tie dye shirts and floppy bell bottomed trousers were the current uniform. Iowa City was also like this , but less so. The language was full of ridiculous words such as "cool," "far out," and "awesome" ("I'm like" had not yet entered the current language), and we were criticized for looking too straight. When Hugh and I were on campus one day, two "hippies" came up to us to get our signature on an anti-war petition. One said, "don't bother with them, they are too straight!" We supported their petition, but they didn't approach us. The hippies were very intolerant of straight-looking people. We went on many anti-war marches and demonstrations and gave out anti-war literature, but we didn't fit into the new culture. We were appalled by the window smashing of businesses and merchants on University Avenue "because their taxes went to the war effort" and with other excesses of the anti-war culture.

Bar Mitzvahs

Ralph was the first to prepare for a Bar Mitzvah, and he had a terrific tutor who came to our house and inspired all of us. As a consequence, we all joined a Hebrew language course at Lehrhaus Judaica, which was housed in the Hillel building right across from Boalt Law School. The teachers, Irene Resnikoff and Linda Israeli, were terrific, and they accepted our mixed age family into their classes. It was a lot of work to study Hebrew, but it was well worth it, as the kids did magnificently at their B'nai Mitzvot services. Ralph set a high bar for the kids at Beth El. The families at the center bonded and became fast friends, as we all participated in cooking and preparing for the *Kiddush* (after Shabbat Services) lunches for the other Bar/Bat Mitzvahs to follow, and for hosting the parties after the services. I was terrified that the kids wouldn't be well prepared, but they all did magnificently. The preparations were stressful but led to wonderful results. The kids learned their *Parashot* (Torah portion for the week) and blessings, read from the Torah, and gave wonderful speeches. They showed that they had real insight in their *Parashot* and we, the parents, learned a lot.

Laila's Bat Mitzvah, which was five years after Joel's, was spectacular. She was extremely well prepared, poised and charming, and we were very proud of her. She learned two different styles of chants for her portion, "Miriam's Song at the

Sea" and Deborah's (the General) song after her success at battle. We were astonished at the high level of Laila's achievement, and the Cantor was so impressed that he wrote a beautiful recommendation for a scholarship to a 10th grade program at a Hebrew High School in Israel, Kfar Blum.

Bringing Opa (Grandpa Sami) to Berkeley

Hugh and I had a scheme to bring my father, the kids' Opa (Grandpa), to Berkeley. He was reluctant to leave Middletown, NY, where he had been a senior psychiatrist at the Middletown State Hospital. He resisted the move strenuously and did not want to leave the area where my mother was buried. I certainly empathized with his wishes, but it was obvious that he was aging and getting frail. He had several falls on the ice during the winters, and we were concerned about his living alone, eating properly, not being able to drive, and being retired with nothing to do. Hugh and I decided to kidnap him by bringing him to Ralph's Bar Mitzvah in 1973. Hugh planned to go the American Physical Society' meeting in New York, and he used that as an excuse to visit my father and have him accompany him on the flight home to Berkeley. Hugh had also engaged a moving company to pack up my dad's household, and I rented a very nice two-room complex at the Shattuck Hotel in downtown Berkeley.

The Shattuck Hotel was centrally located, near banks, department stores, the library and the post office and, best of all, was within walking distance of the UC campus. The Shattuck had a very distinguished clientele of retired UC faculty members, and Dad joined a group of these classically trained professors every evening to discuss the news and politics. After the initial shock of being forcefully moved across the country wore off, he adjusted beautifully and joined a group of doctors, who were members of congregation Beth El, to go on medical rounds at Alta Bates Hospital, that thrilled him. He audited courses in biochemistry and genetics at UC Berkeley. Dad often went to coffee shops with students who were delighted to meet an "old world" doctor who had studied with giants of the medical profession such as Alois Altzheimer, who discovered plaques in the brains of dementia patients, and he entertained the students with anecdotes about his former professors.

The Shattuck hotel was within walking distance of Berkeley High School, so our kids were able to visit Opa after school, when he would take them out for ice cream at Eddies, the local ice cream parlor. It was a very nice experience for all of them. To my amazement, several older ladies at the Beth El Congregation made friends with Opa and seemed to be "interested" in him, but he didn't fall for any of them. He was very loyal to my mother.

Dad was obsessed with his research on the anti-oxidant enzyme, superoxide dismutase. There wasn't a single conversation that he had with me in which he didn't discuss his theories about the function of this enzyme. It now appears that there is a genetic underpinning of this enzyme in ALS sufferers (Lou Gehrig's disease). He had a great intellectual bent for science and medical diagnostics. I am amazed at how prescient he was in medical sciences. He felt that the underlying causes of mental illnesses were biological, not environmental. My opinion is that it is a combination of both.

We invited Opa to dinner every Friday evening and to all Jewish holidays and family events. He was happy to be a part of our family and observe his grandchildren's development. He had mellowed out with age and was pleasant to be with, even though he was still very eccentric.

At that time, the Reform services were very bland, and Beth El even featured an organ, just as in churches, and it became very uncomfortable for our family. We moved to a newly formed Conservative Synagogue, Netivoth Shalom, and about ten years later, we joined the Orthodox congregation, Beth Israel, whose Rabbi was highly inspiring. I still attend Beth Israel.

My Job Hunt

Once the kids were settled in school, I redoubled my efforts to find a job in my chosen field. I haunted the job offices at UC Berkeley but found nothing except for several unpaid internships. I accepted an internship in San Francisco in a genetics lab, which didn't work out. The commuting, an unpleasant supervisor, long hours and lack of pay were not compatible with my job expectations.

I heard of an interesting and newly established program at UC Berkeley called Genetic Counseling, that I investigated. The program admitted only six students, and I decided to apply. I had training in genetics, but I had no counseling experience, which the program stressed. The program directors felt they could more easily teach genetics to students who had psychology or counseling backgrounds, rather than teach counseling to geneticists.

One of the items in the application was a request to write an essay on personal experiences with heritable diseases. I carry a gene for Tay-Sacks disease, a lethal neurological illness found in Ashkenazi (Eastern European) Jews. Two such mutant alleles in an embryo would lead to the expression of the disease and result in death of the child. I also had an uncle with Down syndrome, who was murdered by the Nazis in their "racial purification" program. In my essay, I expressed my opinion that only the parents of a baby who showed a positive prenatal diagnosis of heritable diseases should be allowed to make the decision of terminating the pregnancy, not the state. I was horrified by the Nazi's euthanasia program and felt that the state must not interfere with the parents' decision.

I received a letter of rejection from a member of the admissions committee saying that I was "too involved in my ethnic origins" to belong in the program. At that time the other well known heritable genetic condition for which there was prenatal screening was sickle cell anemia, a devastating blood disease often found in Mediterranean and African communities. In the hybrid state, the gene confers resistance to malaria but produces no sickle cell anemia. In the case of two mutant sickle cell alleles, the child would have the full blown and terrible disease. There are many sickle cell carriers and sufferers in the United States, and African Americans were concerned about a euthanasia program. The admissions committee did not seem to find that ethnic (racial) considerations interfered with the acceptance of black applicants, although it rejected mine. It seemed to be a double standard. In retrospect, I probably would not have been a good counselor because I felt that if I were carrying a fetus with genes for a terrible disease I would choose to terminate the pregnancy and would have felt very frustrated by parents who did not share my view.

BIOTECH - A Job At Last

I answered an ad for the very first biotech company, Cetus Corporation. The company was located in Berkeley, and its program was to cultivate the microorganism that would produce high levels of the antibiotic, Gentamycin. The scientific board of directors included the Nobel Laureate for Physics (1960), Dr. Donald Glaser, who had invented the bubble chamber in 1952 for use in subatomic particle physics. The members of the scientific board of directors were all well-known scientists, and I decided to apply. To my surprise, I was offered a job because part of my graduate thesis was on the genetics of antibiotic resistance. It was a perfect fit. The employees were all affiliated with UCB, and Cetus had the atmosphere of an academic department. I would have preferred an academic career, but this was pretty fantastic.

My job was routine at first but became more interesting as the company grew and branched out into novel areas of cancer diagnostics, cancer cures and developing genetic analyses for various heritable diseases. Cetus developed a number of exciting new therapies to treat cancer, specifically the interleukins (immune modulators,) and I was lucky to be able join a department that was developing cancer markers, groundbreaking cancer diagnostics and cancer therapies. I helped develop a diagnostic procedure for detecting prostate cancer involving simultaneous assays for Prostatic Specific Antigen (PSA) and Bone Alkaline Phosphatase (BAP) for which my name was put on the Cetus patent. For this effort in helping develop the assays I received the princely sum of $2.00. The scientists and assistants were a friendly bunch, and I felt very comfortable at Cetus, at least during the first few years. I made some wonderful friends at Cetus and many of them are still close to me today.

As the company grew, it became very corporate, with administrators who were not scientists and did not know how to maintain a creative atmosphere. I stayed at Cetus for 17 years and was involved with many significant scientific projects including oil biochemistry, cancer diagnostics, immunotherapy and Cetus's most famous invention, the Polymerase Chain Reaction (PCR), that was invented and developed by Dr. Karry Mullis who received the Nobel Prize for his invention. PCR is now an essential tool in biological research and is a standard part of every biology lab. Archeologists, forensic scientists, epidemiologists, genomics and all kinds of medical researchers use PCR in scientific research.

Catastrophic Diagnosis of Breast Cancer

Our family went on our annual vacation to Ashland, Oregon, for its Shakespeare Festival when I was 41 years old. We stayed in a campground and I was excited to start a wonderful vacation. While I was lathering up in the shower my hands felt a lump in my right breast and I suddenly went numb. That morning I had read an article in the newspaper about both Betty Ford's and Shirley Temple Black's breast cancers and the need for self-examinations to "catch" the cancer while it was still small. I would have never even thought about cancer if I had not read those articles. I had received a negative mammogram less than four months before the startling discovery of my lump. I immediately suspected that my lump was quickly growing cancer and ran out of the shower, hair still soaped up, and told Hugh to drive me to the hospital immediately. Hugh was calm and soothing and told me to go back into the shower and finish washing my hair. He promised to take me to a doctor as soon as possible.

We went to the local small hospital but the physician on duty was a dermatologist who referred me to a general practitioner. I was so panicked that I made an immediate visit to the general practitioner. He suggested that the lump was probably a cyst that he could drain, all would be well and he would be my hero. The bad news was that it was a solid tumor, and he told me to make an appointment with my Berkeley doctor after my vacation. The vacation was ruined for me! I tried to sit through the Shakespeare plays and not talk about my problem in order not to worry the kids, but I can't even remember the names of the plays. Somehow, I kept it all together until we all returned home.

I went straight to my family doctor, and he immediately referred me to a surgeon who was in the same complex. While I waited for the receptionist to confirm my appointment, my mouth was dry that I couldn't read, the wait was agonizing. Finally, after two hours, I timidly asked the receptionist to which doctor I was supposed to go. She had completely forgotten about me and told me to hurry to Dr. Killen, the surgeon, and I hurried to his office. His waiting room was full of very sick-looking people, which made me even more anxious. After he examined me he told me that he had a slot open for me to have a biopsy the following afternoon at Alta Bates Hospital. He explained that if the lump were benign, he would simply remove it, but if the pathologist saw suspicious cells in the section, he would do a mastectomy immediately. There was to be no time in between biopsy and surgery. I agreed to this horrible proposal and went home to tell Hugh. Joel was in summer camp and Ralph had a summer job in Dr. David Freifelder's lab at Brandeis in Boston, so I had only to find an arrangement for Laila during my hospital stay. I had to be prepared for either a very short, or long, hospitalization and keep up my spirits for either outcome.

The next day Hugh dropped me off at the hospital, and I was shocked that my father was already in the waiting room. He tried to reassure me, but he was obviously even more anxious as I was. The anesthesiologist visited me and explained what was to happen in surgery the next morning. I tried to sleep that night but I had fantasies all night of leaving Hugh a widower with three children. This kind of pessimism and negativity is typical of me and has plagued me all of my life. Hugh was at my side when I awoke from surgery and he told me I had not undergone a mastectomy so I was very relieved. Hugh explained that I was scheduled for bone and liver scans to see if the malignancy had spread and, only after a thorough examination, would I have the mastectomy. I was shocked but later heartened when no metastases were found and was relieved that I was going to have that dreaded mastectomy after all. I told my father the news, and he remarked that perhaps I might survive longer than my oncologist. That is what he had learned to say when he was in medical school. Ironically, Dr. Killen died in a fall six months later.

After the mastectomy and hospital stay, I was scheduled to have what was, at that time, a series of treatments with a new chemotherapy cocktail called CMF (Cytoxan, Methotrexate and 5-Fluorouracil) for twelve monthly cycles, to destroy any micrometastases because I had a positive axillary node. WOW! Was I going to be sick for a year? Would I live? I decided that I was going to fight like hell and get through this, continue working and live a meaningful life. I was worried about how Hugh was going to accept my mutilated body, but I needn't have. Hugh was kind, loving and supportive and was not even shocked when he saw my scar. I cried when I showed Hugh my flat chest with the long from shoulder to waist, scar, but he just said that he loved me and that I would get well.

To my surprise, one of my boys offered some marijuana for my nausea. I had been quite sick from the chemo and needed relief. I was shocked by his offer, but decided to try to eat some of it, as I don't smoke. Unfortunately, it didn't help after all, but I can say that I tried some marijuana. I will tell my grandchildren.

A breast cancer survivor who belonged to a cancer support group visited me in the hospital. She gave me some useful advice about how to construct a bra to balance the flat side (now there are many great models of commercial orthopedic bras) and a good diet to get me through the nausea of chemo sickness. She was very kind but was ultimately not very helpful. One of the most maddening comments was if I cultivated a good attitude, it would help me cure the cancer. I know that people meant well, but these comments implied that if I had a recurrence it was my own fault for having a bad attitude. It seems to imply that the well-wisher had a good attitude, that kept her well and my cancer was the result of my "bad" attitude. I wanted to smash them in the face, but I usually just thanked my friends for their good wishes. They meant no harm, but it made me furious. Anyhow, despite my worries and bad attitude, I survived the cancer.

Life Goes On

I took a month's leave from my job to recover from the surgery, but I did not take a single day of sick leave during the 12 cycles of chemotherapy. The chemo lasted a few extra months, because my blood count did not rise to the proper level between scheduled appointments, but I eventually got through the treatments. I lost my hair, which fell out during my second month of chemo and completely stopped up the drain in the shower. I screamed when most of the hair just fell out, but Hugh just got the "snake" and reamed out the drain and, the next day, drove me to a wig shop. I bought a wig that I never used and finally gave to Laila to use for her Halloween witch costume. The next year I sewed some toy rubber snakes in it and she went as Medusa. So much for the wig! After my chemo was over and a short wait, I had reconstructive breast surgery, which made me feel much better about myself. The reconstruction went without incident but was only about half the size of my other breast, so I was quite asymmetrical. I was proud of the fact that I didn't miss a beat during that time, now 42 years ago.

Ralph graduated Berkeley High and went on to UC Berkeley to study physics and applied math, Joel was busy with high school, hang gliding and singing bass in the Berkeley High chorus. Laila was in middle school and was working very hard on her ballet classes and preparing for her Bat Mitzvah. Life went on as normally as possible. I was very anxious about my recovery and felt terrible about my mutilated body. I felt that I was no longer a sexually desirable woman and was depressed. Thankfully the kids were all very busy at this time. Laila was cast as Clara in the Nutcracker ballet at the Berkeley Ballet and Joel had a job working for our next-door neighbor who was the *Chronicle* delivery person for the Berkeley Hills. Joel had to collate the sections of thousands of Sunday *Chronicle* newspapers (an all-night job). Ralph was attending UC Berkeley as a physics and applied math major and lived in a dorm. He also had a part-time job at Cetus, doing various technical jobs.

One afternoon Joel was riding his bicycle on Grizzly Peak Boulevard and was hit by a car. The driver stopped, picked him up, drove him and the bicycle to the hospital and then drove off without leaving his name. Joel had a broken arm, a broken nose and a severely cut lip. A surgeon sewed him up, but a nerve in his lip was damaged and his embouchure was ruined. He could not play the clarinet anymore and had to leave the school orchestra, but he joined the chorus as a bass singer. The chorus experience was great, and it even toured Europe. About six weeks later Joel broke his nose again at soccer practice, and his surgeon was furious that he had to re-set his nose.

The Emigration of the Soviet Jews

Hugh and I became involved with the plight of Soviet Jews in the 1980's and we went to demonstrations at the Soviet Embassy in San Francisco on a weekly basis. In the '80's there was a very strong movement in the U.S. to try to let the Soviet Jews immigrate to Israel or the USA. We joined a committee to help those Jews to immigrate and we were able to help find apartments, show them how to use bank accounts and to write resumes so that they could obtain jobs in their professions. We were very lucky to be assigned several families whom we could help. It was wonderful to get to know the immigrants and we made good friends with many of them.

Cuban Jews

We became very concerned about the fate of Cuban Jews who were out of contact with mainstream Jewry because of the U.S. boycott of Cuba. Through the efforts of our good friend, June Safran, we were able to join a group to visit Cuba to join a medical mission deliver medical supplies to Cuba's Jewish community.

We flew from Miami to Havana with suitcases loaded with medications and Jewish prayer books and were treated to a wonderful reception by the Jewish Community. Most of our stay was in Santiago de Cuba where there was a small but vigorous Jewish community. We were overwhelmed with their generous hospitality even though conditions were very difficult. We were invited to dinner at the Synagogue in Santiago de Cuba and the main dish was spaghetti. Our mission members received the spaghetti with sauce, but the community members ate theirs plain.

We were amazed by the Jewish community in Havana's ability to conduct a service without prayer books. The congregation had memorized the entire service in Hebrew, an amazing feat.

Cetus' Law Suit Lawsuit Against Stanford

During my time at Cetus, I helped train a postdoctoral fellow, a Stanford medical doctor, Dr. Mark Colodny, who was working on infectious diseases in the PCR techniques. He returned to Stanford and developed a diagnostic test for the AIDS virus, and Stanford applied for a patent.

Eventually Cetus was split and sold to two new biotech companies, Roche West and Chiron, but not all of the employees were retained by new companies. I was on vacation when the breakup occurred and was unable to compete for the jobs at either of the new companies, so I was jobless after 17 years with Cetus. I felt very angry, hurt and disappointed.

Several years after I was laid off, Stanford and Cetus (later, Roche West) became entangled in a patent dispute over the diagnostic test for the AIDS virus, and my notebooks were used to justify Cetus' (now Roche's) patent position. I was deposed and, based in part on the experiments described in my notebooks, Roche won the patent rights in the US Supreme Court. I was not notified about the win nor was I compensated for the time I spent reviewing the notebooks or giving my deposition. I was simply treated as old furniture – thrown out.

Xoma Corporation

I found position as an associate scientist at a very mediocre biotechnology company named Xoma, that had a novel approach to cancer therapy, using monoclonal antibody therapy. Xoma was developing a monoclonal antibody for a drug to treat melanoma. Xoma's therapy did not succeed, and I was assigned to do very boring and routine "quality control" analyses. I worked at Xoma for seven years during which I developed many new and accurate assays for new treatment medications for cancer that were being developed, in addition to the routine assays. The work assignments became more interesting but came to a halt when a new department chairman was hired.

At the end of my seven years, Xoma recruited a new manager for our department who had a business degree but no scientific expertise. I had developed a new assay for our new product that did not require radioactive isotopes—detection was based on a colorimetric assay, which could be prepared for a year's supply, divide and frozen so that we would have a reproducible, non-isotopic, reliable assay. This technique would save the company huge amounts of money because we would not need to have a license for weekly purchases of radioactive isotopes and would not require a storage facility to allow the isotopes to decay for several years. The new assay would constitute a reliable method and, most importantly, would save money in the long run. The new manager rejected my approach, because he felt the initial cost of a special scanner would add too large a cost to our quarterly department budget, and he was only interested in the quarterly "bottom line." Over a year, the cost would have been a great deal lower than the cost of the current procedure. The manager rejected my proposal, resented my input, and shortly afterwards I was fired over a trivial matter. I sued Xoma and won a pitifully small settlement.

Our Daughter Laila

Our third child, Laila Ruth, was an adorable daughter who was born in 1967, the year of the so-called "Summer of Love." She was beautiful and was adored by everyone in our family. Ralph and Joel played with their little sister and, aside from a little bit of teasing, were wonderful big brothers, and she loved them. Laila was lively and vivacious and loved to do somersaults on the sidewalk. She enjoyed nursery school and had many friends who frequently came to our house. I loved having a little daughter who was lively, artistic, talented and affectionate.

Ballet

Laila became fascinated by ballet when she was five years old and wanted to take dance lessons, so we enrolled her in a ballet school in Berkeley. She excelled in dance and longed for more classes, and soon she was going five times per week to dance class. She seemed to be musical and was always on the beat and soon started to join more advanced classes. Ballet became an obsession, and as a result she lost some interest in schoolwork, but she was smart and did fairly well in school. We encouraged her in her passion for dance, and she had lots of friends who participated in the long rehearsals and extra classes. They would often come and spend the evenings and stay for overnights at our house. Laila was cast as Clara in the seasonal production of the Nutcracker, which was a big thrill for all of us. What was especially nice was that my mother's name was Klara. Hugh became a "Ballet Dad" who hauled the girls and their ballet equipment around to rehearsals and performances. He also installed a huge mirror in Laila's room and built her a *barre* so she could practice her exercises at home. It was huge fun for us to have such happy and delightful daughter.

Laila at 4 years of age posing with an ice-cream
cone

Laila's Activities

Laila was very active and eagerly went to Hebrew School and to Jewish summer camps. She loved swimming, dancing and art programs at camp. She also came with us on many of our camping trips to the Sierra Mountains and joined in with our annual summer camping trips to Ashland, where we saw Shakespeare plays. She was always busy and had many friends and was well liked, especially by her best friend, Odille, and her other ballet classmates. She always invited the least popular kids in her class to her birthday parties, in order to make them feel liked and welcomed. Hugh took her on exciting river rafting trips. Laila was an artistic, sensitive, empathetic and athletic young girl.

Laila's Bat Mitzvah

After Laila's Bat Mitzvah, in which she did beautifully under the tutelage of her close teacher Irene Resnikoff, she started to lose interest in school and even ballet. We attributed this to the usual teen-age blues, but her moodiness and her attitude became a problem. She made friends with a young girl whose parents were on sabbatical in Berkeley from Scotland. Her new girlfriend had two older siblings who attended Berkeley High School, and they often invited the two girls to their social activities. We were not aware of it at the time, but Berkeley High was a cesspool of drugs. Laila was introduced to drugs at the parties filled with older kids. Her personality changed from cheerful to moody, defiant and rebellious. We were unable to convince her to do schoolwork, clean her room, come home in the evenings, or even be a happy camper. We were completely stumped.

The boys went through adolescence and that period was challenging. Joel's passion was hang gliding and skate boarding, both very dangerous sports. He came home from a hang gliding weekend and asked me what altitude I thought that he had achieved on his flight. I guessed "two thousand feet." Joel informed me that he had flown to 14,000 feet, the altitude that airplanes fly. He descended when he was freezing and found it difficult to breathe. Ralph's passion was chess and at least that was not dangerous, a great relief.

Joel's employer was our next door neighbor who delivered the San Francisco Chronicle to Berkeley Hills' subscribers. He was a difficult person to get along with and we had many conflicts, in part because he had a fleet of 13 cars that lined our narrow and winding street. Some years after the boys had married and moved away, my neighbor and I got into a huge conflict when I accidentally sprayed water on him when I was watering the shrubs between our houses. He called the police and accused me of battering him and the cops arrested me and I went to the Berkeley jail. After being fingerprinted, handcuffed and frisked I was put into a jail cell. It happened to be Joel's birthday and we had planned a family dinner at a restaurant. I explained this to the police and they allowed me to leave for the family dinner provided that I return afterwards. After dinner I explained to the grandkids that I had to leave to go back to jail and went back to the station that was closed. I went to the back door and rang the bell and finally a policeman appeared and asked me what I wanted. I replied, "I want to go back to jail" and he was astonished. After an hour in a holding cell he told me to go home and I would be called by the district attorney. I went home and never heard from the DA.

Laila's Problems

We realized that Laila was having more difficulties than we had previously imagined and we didn't know how to cope with them. There was a program in Israel called "Tenth Grade High School in Israel" which she seemed excited about, and we urged her to apply. She received a scholarship and left for a year at Kibbutz Kfar Blum in the upper Galilee near the Lebanese border. I visited her at her Kibbutz, and she seemed to be happy and had made friends with her group who were mostly from the

US and Canada. I thought that things were getting better. I liked what I saw—happy thriving Zionist teenagers, an academically oriented school, and students who were having great social and cultural experiences. Laila was "adopted" by a host family on the Kibbutz and was well integrated into their home. Laila and I took several wonderful trips to see family, friends, and many architectural, geographical and Biblical sights.

The War with Lebanon

The Lebanese-Israeli war broke out while the visiting students were on the Kibbutz. Kfar Bloom was designated as a rest and recreation station for the Israeli soldiers who had crossed back over the border into Israel, and the Israeli kids had the job of doing their laundry and feeding them. There was a *New York Times* reporter on assignment who interviewed Laila. She was delighted and excited that her quotes were in the Times. All of the students had to sleep and study in the bomb shelters, and they were disappointed that they had to take their final exams during the war. The Principal told them that "life goes on-even during wartime." That is the reality in Israel.

We Hosted an Israeli Student

I thought things were going well. I signed up to be a host family for an Israeli High School student to come and live with us for a semester, so that there would be some continuity to Laila's Hebrew language studies, and she would have an interesting "sister" for the coming year. We welcomed Karina, a delightful

17-year-old student, who wanted to study for the Reform Rabbinate.

Laila returned from Israel and seemed delighted to have an Israeli "sister" in our home for the semester. They both enrolled into the eleventh-grade program at Berkeley High School and took similar classes. Our foster daughter, Karina, became a teaching assistant at the Midrasha, the Jewish post-Bar Mitzvah program, and Laila attended Midrasha and took ballet classes after school. I resolved to avoid school issues and let her work them out herself and to concentrate on my job and having fun with the girls.

Berkeley High School

Things didn't work out as well as I had hoped. Hugh was in Japan for two months as a visiting professor, while I was working at Cetus and hosting Karina, a charming and intelligent 11th grader, originally from Brazil. The girls got along with each other, but Laila fell into her old habit of hating school and eventually stopped going altogether. Hugh was in Japan, so I did not have his help or support. One day I received a notice that Laila had not been in school for three weeks. I was furious for the school's failing to notify me earlier. I asked Laila about attending school and her response was to run away from home. I was terrified and feared that she would drop out of school completely. Fortunately, she returned but was sullen and uncooperative. I did not know how to help her.

Drugs, Mainly Amphetamines

Laila's was born in 1967 just two weeks before the first "Human Be-In" in San Francisco. The message of the "Be-In" was supposed to be of love and camaraderie, but it turned into a gathering of as many as 100,000 young people sporting hippie fashions of dress and behavior that included a life style of sex, drugs, and rock and roll, and anti-establishment behavior. Its legacy, which included drugs, influenced Laila's generation and her life style, including drugs, destroyed her. It was terrifying to watch Laila change from being a delightful and happy person to being hostile and dysfunctional.

After Hugh returned from Japan and Karina went back to Israel, we realized that we had a huge problem. We tried family therapy, individual therapy, tutoring, more supervision and then less supervision. We wanted to be flexible and understanding and not be manipulative. Laila stopped going to her ballet classes. One day Laila told me that she was sick and was having a heart attack, so I drove her to the emergency room where the attending physician informed me that she was overdosing on methamphetamines, which was which was causing her heart to race. I was shocked and in despair.

PACT

I read in the local newspaper that there was a newly formed group of desperate parents trying to cope with children who were out of control: dropping out of school, dropping into drugs. The group was called Parents and Children Together (PACT). I called the number and started attending group meetings with people who I thought had some answers. It was comforting to know that we were not the only parents who had children with drug problems. The other parents, who were also in despair, had visited a number drug rehab centers, and they produced a booklet with a list of local treatment programs. The group had a "tough love" attitude, in style at the time, but with which I now disagree. I also disagreed with the theory that the addicts would not respond to treatment until they hit "bottom." Hugh and I were confused and desperate. We had no experience with drugs, and were influenced by PACT's philosophy.

First Hospitalization

We forced Laila into a drug treatment program for teens at a hospital on the Peninsula. Laila was just short of her 18th birthday, almost the age where her consent was needed. On her 18th birthday, January 4th, 1985, she ran away from the unlocked rehab center and hitchhiked to San Francisco. She got as far as Golden Gate Park where she was picked up by the police because she looked like a runaway. We were called at about 3:00 AM and drove to the police station, where she was shackled to two steel poles. We were told that they had never had a teenager who had struggled so much. She refused to speak to us, and we negotiated indirectly through a policeman, who finally persuaded her to get into our car, provided that we would take her where she wanted to go. She requested to be taken to an address in Emeryville where a friend of hers was staying. We had no choice but to take her there. The police department had no reason to hold her, and she refused to return home. It was a horrendous night.

Attendant Jobs

After leaving the rehab, Laila found a job taking care of a severely handicapped and bedridden woman with whom she lived for a while. But the woman's adult son tried to molest Laila, so she left that job. After that, she had a series of attendant jobs for handicapped people. She was able to live with some patients, but not all. This period of Laila's life was very stressful for us, but we admired her pluck to take such difficult and low paying jobs. She could have just lived at home, gone to school, and enjoyed all kinds of advantages. What we did not understand was that because she was a drug addict, our messages to her were all scrambled up in her addicted brain. We had no experience with this and did not know what to do. We were terrified.

Himalayan Trek

In 1987, we attended The Himalayan Fair, run by our neighbor, biochemist and mountaineer, Dr. Arlene Blum. She had led and climbed Mt. Annapurna in an all-women's expedition. Arlene was organizing another expedition, and I asked Laila if she wanted to go for a month of mountaineering in Nepal. This thrilled her, and she decided to apply. We hoped that strenuous exercise in an exotic place might help her. The night before she was to join the trek, she was arrested for drawing graffiti downtown. We were called by the police who held her passport, which she had taken with her. Hugh bailed her out and retrieved her passport from the police, and she managed to join the expedition at the airport early in the morning. Laila did well on the trek, which reached the level of 18,000 feet, because she was an excellent athlete. She loved Nepal and decided to live in Katmandu for a while. We had mixed feelings about this, but we decided to allow her to stay in Nepal.

Nepal

Laila's visa expired after a few months, and she needed to leave and then re-enter Nepal to extend her visa. She crossed the Nepalese border and went to India, planning on returning to Nepal the next day. Laila did not realize was that she needed to stay in India for several months before being able to return to Nepal. She had no resources fort this, so she bribed a Nepalese border guard and was readmitted to Nepal. We received a phone call from the American embassy in Katmandu, saying that Laila had come to the embassy with a young Afghan man who wanted to marry her. The embassy employee suspected that the intention of the Afghan man was to get a US visa and green card, and the employee called to inform us of what was going on. The embassy refused to issue the man a US visa, and the marriage of convenience did not occur.

Dog Bite

Laila was bitten by a dog in Katmandu and she feared the dog might have rabies. The Nepalese government agreed to arrange for recombinant anti-rabies shots, for which we were extremely grateful. At this time, Hugh received an invitation to New Zealand and Australia to give a series of lectures on the necessity of stopping atmospheric nuclear testing and creating an international nuclear disarmament agreement. We contacted Laila and convinced her to come home, with the inducement of taking her on our "down under" trip for a month. We obtained anti-rabies vaccine from the California Department of Public Health so that she could continue with her vaccinations, and the three of us set off on a month-long trip to New Zealand and Australia.

New Zealand and Australia

We were met at the airport by a lovely couple, Dr. Brian and Anne Davis, at whose home we stayed, and with whom we are still close friends. Hugh gave his lectures, and Laila and I were able to tour New Zealand and get to know something about the aboriginal culture and see the wonderful country and its millions of sheep. Laila was erratic and would disappear at times, but the NZ stay was generally pleasant. Hugh was able to deliver his lectures on "The Nuclear Test Ban" to large and receptive audiences. We flew to Australia, where we had the same warm and friendly hospitality, and we stayed at several homes and made good and long-lasting friendships. Hugh continued to give lectures at several universities and political groups, and Laila and I enjoyed exploring Sydney, Melbourne, Canberra and several other cities. The people were very welcoming, and Hugh's talks were well attended. I am sure that the Lawrence Livermore lab's directors were appalled at Hugh's political activities. Imagine, one of their employees talking about ending nuclear testing in the world! Laila and I returned home before Hugh because my vacation time was used up, but Hugh continued on his tour and went to Tasmania to complete his lectures.

Hugh was still greatly involved in his astrophysics research and continued to serve as an editor and reviewer for many journals. He drove to the Livermore Laboratory daily and continued on in his thriving professional career. I devoted myself to pro-Israel activities and e-published my Israel-activist Newsletter three times per week to a huge subscription list. I attended every pro-Israel event or lecture that was available and went to political meetings and events.

Central America and The Galapagos

Hugh and I took some trips that were not related to his professional work. One of our trips was to the Galapagos, an experience that validated my acceptance and excitement about evolution. We flew to Guatemala, south of Mexico, and continued on to the islands of the Galapagos where Charles Darwin, centuries ago, observed the animals and plants present on the islands. His observations led to his understanding of the origin of species and how the variations developed. I was fascinated by the blue-footed Boobies who allowed us to walk right by their nests and who flew to the sea to catch fish. We met Lonesome George, the last tortoise of his species, who had no consort. The lava beds were the home for many species that don't exist anywhere else but the Galapagos. I was very surprised that there were equatorial penguins living in the islands. I had believed that these birds existed only in the Antarctic. Anyone who doubts evolution should take a trip to the Galapagos.

Hugh's Involvement with The Progressive Case (1979)

While I was driving to work on day in 1979, I heard a news broadcast on NPR about a legal case in which the US Government was issuing a "Prior Restraint" order against the publication of an article by *The Progressive* Magazine called "The Secret of the Hydrogen Bomb," written by journalist Howard Morland. The U.S. government argued that the article contained classified information about nuclear weapons development. I told Hugh about the injunction against the magazine, and he immediately understood the urgency of challenging the government's attempt to interfere with freedom of the press. Hugh had security clearance at The Lawrence Livermore Labs (LLL) and was acquainted with nuclear weapons development, so he contacted Sam Day, editor of *The Progressive*, and offered his services to help show that there was nothing classified in Morland's article. This action catapulted our lives into a vigorous attack by Livermore and the government.

Sam Day was delighted to have someone of Hugh's stature and prestige in the physics community who had the necessary understanding and classification status who would volunteer to work with him to try to get the "Prior Restraint" order lifted. Sam flew to the Bay Area from Wisconsin and met Hugh at a motel to read the Morland article. Sam and Hugh did not want to meet at our house, because such a meeting might come to the attention of the government and would compromise them. Hugh told me that he would return in about an hour but, after about three hours had gone by, I became very nervous and anxious that something had gone wrong. He finally reappeared and told me that he had read the article, saw nothing that was classified in it, and would write an affidavit to the court saying that everything that appeared in the article was already in the public domain, printed in the *Encyclopedia Britannica*, in an article written by Dr. Edward Teller, the director of the Lawrence Livermore Lab. Hugh said that any physics student could go to the encyclopedia and be able to understand the article. He recognized that the "Born Secret" doctrine was a potent suppressor of free speech on a subject of immense importance, and that the information had been on public shelves for some time.

A lawsuit was brought against *The Progressive* by the United States Department of Energy (DOE) in 1979, and a temporary injunction was granted against *The Progressive* to prevent the publication of the article by Howard Morland, which purported to reveal the "secret" of the hydrogen bomb. Though the information had been compiled from publicly available sources, the DOE claimed that it fell under the "Born Secret" clause of the Atomic Energy Act of 1954.

The cover of the Progressive magazine:

I recently cleaned out my basement and found several T-shirts with "The H-Bomb Secret" cover stenciled on them. They had been made as a fund-raiser for *The Progressive*, and I had stashed away a few to give to our grandchildren. I had already given our children some of the T-shirts, and Hugh and I marched around Berkeley, proudly wearing them. We received a lot of stares.

Few of Hugh's colleagues dared come out publicly to defend Hugh, as it seemed very dangerous for LLNL scientists to do so and come to the attention and wrath of their supervisors and the directors. One of the few exceptions was Dr. Ray Kidder who had been a nuclear weapons designer at Livermore and Los Alamos. Kidder was able to credibly dispute government arguments in the battle of affidavits, leveling the technical playing field. Because of the importance of radiation implosion in civilian fusion research, Ray had been quietly waging a campaign to declassify it for some years prior to *The Progressive* case.

Things became incredibly complicated, but Hugh persisted, mailing his affidavit to the court, testifying that the article was not a threat to national security and that it contained no classified information. The document that Hugh wrote was automatically classified, as are all papers emanating from the Lab, and it had to go through a "declassification procedure" before being transmitted to the Wisconsin court. Hugh carefully followed all procedures to get the necessary signatures to declassify his affidavit and then sent it to the Judge, Robert W. Warren of the States District Court for the Western District of Wisconsin in Madison.

On April 25, 1979, a group of scientists who worked at the Argonne National Laboratory wrote to Senator John Glenn, the Chairman of the United States Senate Subcommittee on Energy, Nuclear Proliferation and Federal Services. They were concerned about information being leaked, in particular by the government's tacit acknowledgement that Morland's bomb design was substantially correct, something that could not otherwise have been deduced from unclassified information. These included the affidavits by the United States Secretary of Defense, Harold Brown, and government expert witness, Jack Rosengren. Copies of the letter were sent to major newspapers but with a cover note explaining that it was for background information and not publication. After about four weeks, the Glenn subcommittee forwarded it to the DOE, which classified it.

Hugh forwarded a copy to Chuck Hansen, a computer programmer from Mountain View, California, who had collected information about nuclear weapons as a hobby. He had run a competition to design an H-bomb, the winner of which would be the first person to have their design classified by the DOE. It now began to occur to him that his hobby might not be legal. On August 27, he wrote a letter to Senator Charles H. Percy detailing how much information he had deduced from publicly available sources. This included his own design—one not as good as Morland's, which Hansen had not seen. Hansen further charged that government scientists—including Edward Teller, Ted Taylor, and George Rathjens—had leaked sensitive information about thermonuclear weapons, for which no action had been taken. In this, Hansen was mistaken: Taylor had indeed been reprimanded, and Teller was not the source of the information that Hansen attributed to him. Hansen made copies of his letter available to several newspapers.

When *The Daily Californian* published excerpts from the Argonne letter on June 11, the DOE obtained a court order to prevent further publication. Undeterred, *The Daily Californian* published the letter in its entirety on June 13. In September, the DOE declared the Hansen letter to be classified and obtained a temporary restraining order prohibiting *The Daily Californian* from publishing it, but the Hansen letter was published by the *Madison Press Connection* on September 16. The government then moved to dismiss their cases against both *The Progressive* and *The Daily Californian* as moot.

Hugh gave an interview to a reporter at *The Daily Cal*, in which he told the UC Berkeley journalist who "the Livermore directors are a bunch of deadheads." Hugh warned the young journalist not to quote him, but she did, and that quote became *The Daily Cal's* headline. Unaware of the publication, Hugh drove to work at Livermore where there was an ominous message for him: "Report to Dr. Edward Teller's office immediately." The resulting meeting was extremely uncomfortable, and Teller was not shy about ripping into Hugh. It was pretty devastating.

The case was eventually dropped, and the Livermore Lab and its directors needed a scapegoat, and that was Hugh

DeWitt. The Livermore lab and its directors never forgave Hugh for his participation in *The Progressive* case. He was referred to as "Burr Under the Saddle," "A Thorn In the Side" and "A Pain in the Ass!" and was even called "A Chamberlain" by lab director Dr. Edward Teller. This was a reference to Prime Minister Neville Chamberlain, who on September 30, 1938, in Munich, signed away the sovereignty of Czechoslovakia over the Sudetenland. Hugh was notified that he had transmitted classified information without having received proper signatures and was punished relentlessly for many years. Livermore threatened to remove his security clearance, gave him minimal pay raises, moved him to an office without windows, curtailed his travel allowance, restricted his visitors, and gave him poor performance reviews.

This harassment made Hugh angry and stubborn, and he became actively involved with groups that were asking for an end to atmospheric nuclear testing, helping widows of men who were in the South Pacific and Nevada who died from being irradiated during atmospheric tests, and working with worldwide organizations whose mission it was to end the nuclear weapons race. He was involved with the Pugwash Conferences to bring together scientists from around the world, the Nuclear Non-proliferation Treaty of 1968, and the Anti-ballistic Treaty. Hugh was invited to many conferences and went on speaking tours all over the world, to convince people and their governments to end nuclear testing.

These activities took an enormous amount of time and energy, and Hugh threw himself into the effort with enormous passion. The down side for our family was that he was rarely at home and, when he was at home, he was always working, giving interviews, and writing about nuclear disarmament. It was wonderful work, but it was time lost to both our family and to his physics. It was hard on the kids and especially on me. We were all worried that he would lose his job, or worse, get indicted for leaking classified material and go to jail.

Hugh's political activity lasted for many years and wore him out. He aged visibly, became very tired, and suffered from heart arrhythmia and insomnia. I was still exhausted from my breast cancer chemotherapy and also had the burden of the household, because Hugh was completely involved with his political activities. When he had it, he used his time for his plasma physics research. He maintained his "Ballet Dad" activities, however, and ferried Laila's ballet group to rehearsals and performances and delivered ballet *Barres*, props, and costumes, in-between his political activities. During this period, we made many friends in the anti-atmospheric testing movement, and I went along on several exciting trips to Australia, New Zealand, the Soviet Union, Germany, Poland and Britain so that he could meet with his colleagues. He also maintained a vigorous correspondence with his physics collaborators. I was very proud of him, and I was delighted that he had such a meaningful and rich academic and political life.

Hugh had a "garbage can" memory and could recall everything dropped into it. I used him as my personal "Wikipedia," as he knew all kinds of extraordinary facts and was able to recall the details to an astonishing degree. All I had to do was ask, "Hugh, what year was ....?" and I would get an immediate answer, which was correct. I was amazed and astounded at his ability to accurately recall all sorts of important facts.

In 1978 Hugh took a leave of absence from Livermore and spent his year at University of Rochester for the summer session, followed by a semester University of California at Santa Barbara, and finally the spring semester of 1979 at UC Santa Cruz. I decided to stay at my job and not accompany him, but I visited at all three venues for short periods. The stay at Santa Barbara was very productive, and Hugh led an international institute for physics with a group headed by a Nobel Laureate in chemistry, Dr. Walter Kohn. It was a remarkable three months for Hugh, and he thoroughly enjoyed doing physics with world famous scientists. He befriended several colleagues, among them Dr. Wolf Krafft and his wife, Iro, whom we subsequently visited in East Germany several times. I felt very lonely in Berkeley.

The boys were in college and Laila was having major emotional problems. I had a hard time coping with her delinquency and my work problems all by myself.

I was amazed at how hard Hugh worked on both his political and scientific correspondence. I have shelves of Hugh's writings, and I need to have them scanned and archived—a mammoth task. I feel overwhelmed, needing to check through his home computer to assess what needs to be kept or removed. I will have to ask our sons, both physics and math majors, to take care of this chore.

One of the keys to Hugh's character was that he had been an Eagle Scout, of which he was very proud. He was loyal, goal oriented, honest, respectful, loved nature, kind, generous and very hard working. His only flaws were a total lack of rhythm, which made him unable to dance, and his lack of a time sense, which drove me crazy. I had to nag him to get him to events on time, and this led to some irritation and quarreling.

These activities consumed our lives for many years but eventually these frantic times died down and life returned to an almost normal pace. After Hugh passed away in 2014, his close friend, Gerry Marsh, wrote the following words about him:

> "Hugh was a very well-known physicist and his physics contributions were covered in the Physics Today obituary. As I am sure you know, his contributions were not limited to physics. But you may only be partially aware of how important his contributions to public policy were. His defense of the first amendment, balancing the public's need to know against the government's need to protect the information in The Progressive Case was very courageous and cost him personally in many ways. Of equal if not greater importance was his role in contributing to the Star Wars debacle. This story has not yet been fully told, not even in Bill Broad's book, "Teller's War: The Top-Secret Story Behind the Star Wars Deception."

> "One of Hugh's most important contributions involved the Star

Wars program begun by President Reagan in 1983. It is unlikely that this program would have come into existence without the excessive claims made for the nuclear-bomb-pumped x-ray laser, which was central to the program. Yet, it was already known in April 1984 that the sensors that had been used to confirm the lasing were not functioning properly, and there was no clear evidence of lasing. Although the failure was confirmed by a test at Livermore in August 1984, wildly optimistic claims continued to be made as late as 1987. During the intervening years, Hugh played an important role in ensuring that government officials were aware of the deceptive claims coming out of Livermore.

"Without Hugh's help I would have been unable to track the experimental results of the continuing x-ray laser tests. My briefings to high-level government people showing that the x-ray laser didn't exist were a critical factor in its demise. Hugh was also able to inform the JASONs, the review committee responsible for the program, what documents to request from Livermore during their reviews.

"The story of the shameless promotion of the x-ray laser had leaked out because of the frustration of the people involved in the program with the deceptive practices of Edward Teller and the Livermore management in presenting the results in Washington. The leaks got so bad that in 1985 the FBI and Department of Justice were investigating leaks to Bill Broad about the x-ray laser program. I used to have to take the Star Wars program briefing slides and point out the outright hyperbole to people in the Pentagon. It was great fun. But the policy implications of the program, and the staggering waste of money, were not in the least bit funny."

My Volunteer Period in the Israeli Defense forces

I volunteered in the Israeli Defense Forces (IDF) through an organization called Sar El "Volunteers For Israel" that was started by General Davidi in 1982, in order to relieve Israeli forces from routine tasks that volunteers could fill without much training. I was accepted for three weeks of service in November of 2002 and was stationed at a military base near Ramle, an Arab town. The volunteers were integrated into the military base and were housed in cabins together with the regular soldiers. We went to morning flag raisings, wore uniforms, ate in the mess hall as though we were actually in the forces. The volunteers came from many countries and spoke many languages, but we all got along well and were excited by our adventure.

On the first night I needed to use the bathroom and I went in my nightie along the long path to the bathroom hut. On the way I ran into soldiers with assault weapons who barely gave me a glance. I couldn't imagine walking in my nightie in the U.S. and running into guys with machine guns but I felt very safe on base. I was surprised to see many black soldiers who were at the base speaking Hebrew and completely integrated.

My job was to participate in a group that recycled tank helmets and wired them for radio communications. I had to strip off the old earphones, paint the helmets, and rewire them. It was very hot and we worked outside but it was challenging and interesting. The volunteer crews overlapped the new volunteers and taught us how to do the job. I hope that there was quality control to ensure that we accomplished our task correctly. We also refurbished gas masks for school children who were at risk for gas attacks. Our evenings were full of fun and dancing and conversations. There were several organized trips to military establishments and places of interest on weekends and we all saw a great deal of Israel's historical sites.

My Officer and Me, My service in the IDF at the base near Ramle (2002)

After my volunteer service, I took a trip to Hebron on the

day after there was a huge massacre, called an "ambush". I took an armored bus from Jerusalem to Hebron and saw the results of the massacre. The city was teeming with the military and we could not enter the Arab part of the city.

I saw the cemetery of the 1929 massacre of Hebron's Jews that took place long before the State of Israel was established and saw evidence of how intensely the Arabs hated the Jews. I visited a demolished hospital destroyed by an Arab suicide bomber masquerading as a patient.

The Machpelah, the Cave of the Patriarchs where Abraham, Sarah, Rebecca, Isaak and Jacob are buried, is located in Hebron, was liberated in 1967. I had the opportunity to visit and pray in the Machpelah and experience the deep sense of Jewish history. Several of my relatives live in towns near Hebron and I was able to get an extended tour of the area that was very inspiring.

I travelled by bus to the town of Efrat in the Gush Etzion block where I visited close relatives. Efrat, located about eight miles from Jerusalem, is referred to as a settlement in the West but it is simply a town in an area of Israel called Judea Samaria. The word "settlement" has gained a negative political meaning but is located in what was ancient Israel. The location is in dispute with the Palestinians until its status is determined in a final peace agreement. I felt that it was my obligation to explain to my American friends that the location of this town is in Israel and that it should not be regarded as a settlement.

AIPAC Meeting in Washington DC, 2004

I decided to attend as many discussions about the peace talks as possible on my return to the States. I registered for one of the largest pro-Israel conferences in the spring of 2004 that was held in Washington, D.C. The American Israel Policy Conference (AIPAC) is held annually in Washington and attracts over eight thousand attendees. The conference agenda includes parallel sessions with committees and features international speakers including foreign leaders and members of congress or other organizations that are concerned with peace in the Middle East. There were many interesting exhibits and at the 2004 conference it featured the second Intifada.

AIPAC Meeting in Washington DC, 2004

I registered for the AIPAC conference in 2004, and attended daylong sessions for five days. In the Washington Convention Center lobby I saw a striking exhibit of a bombed bus. I was shocked and horrified at the sight of the twisted, shattered bus with all of the windows blown out, and with mangled seats. The sign for the exhibit read: *"The bombing occurred on January 29,*

2004, at 9 a.m., very close to the official residence of Prime Minister Ariel Sharon, who was not in the building at that time." Eleven people died, including the terrorist. The victims were ordinary citizens and tourists who were going to work, to school, or out shopping. Fifty were injured and many of the injuries were very serious.

The bus bombing occurred during the second Intifada between Israel and Palestine, September 28, 2000 to February 8, 2005. The Intifada rose around the time of the Camp David accords when PA authority Chairman Yassir Arafat and Prime Minister Ehud Barak, disagreed about Israel, the so called "occupied Jerusalem" and the declaration of a Palestinian State. Sharon's visit to the Al-Aksa Mosque was followed by violence by the Palestinians including many bus bombings. Jerusalem bus 19 was blown up Jan. 29, 2004, near French Hill.

The Murdered Victims

Avraham (Albert) Balhasan, 28, of Jerusalem (immigrant from France); Rose Boneh, 39, of Jerusalem; Hava Hannah (Anya) Bonder, 38, of Jerusalem (immigrant from Russia); Anat Darom, 23, of Netanya; Viorel Octavian Florescu, 42, of Jerusalem,; Natalia Gamril, 53, of Jerusalem; Yechezkel Isser Goldberg, 41, of Betar Illit (immigrant from Canada); Baruch (Roman) Hondiashvili, 38, of Jerusalem; Dana Itach, 24, of Jerusalem; Mehbere Kifile, 35, of Ethiopia; Eli Zfira, 48, of Jerusalem.

Bus 19 Bombing

Egged Bus 19 (Jerusalem Public Bus) was blown up on January 29, 2004, by Ali Yusuf Jaara, 24, a Palestinian policeman from Bethlehem who was a member of the Al Aqsa Martyrs' Brigades. The homicide bomber packed his explosives with metal shards to maximize injury to the passengers. This marked the 140th homicide BUS bombing. As of 2003, 577 had already been killed in these bombing and 3,543 injured.

The sight of this portable graveyard was a testimony to the

victims of terrorism and a memorial to the innocent people whose lives were destroyed by a suicide bomber. It is a reminder that ordinary civilians who are going about their daily business can become targets, even here in the United States. I was shocked and sickened by the sight of the bombed bus, and I resolved to bring it to Berkeley so that people in the Bay Area could witness the results of terrorism and suicide bombings.

Bringing Bus 19 to Berkeley

FOR THE STOP GLOBAL TERRORISM RALLY ON
SUNDAY, JANUARY 16, 2005 "STOP GLOBAL
TERRORISM" RALLY IN MARTIN LUTHER KING JR.
PARK, BERKELEY, CA

I contacted ZAKA (A Light For Life, www.zaka.org.il), the Israeli organization that does "Rescue and Recovery" for victims of terrorism and is devoted to saving lives by providing emergency rescue services globally, for information on how to bring the bombed bus to Berkeley. ZAKA referred me to Willem Griffioen Jr. of the Christians for Israel, USA, for advice on getting the Terror Bus to Berkeley. He referred me to the Reverend James Hutchings, Brigadier General of the US Army (Retired), whose Christian ministry had brought the bus to the United States. Reverend Hutchings was most gracious and allowed me to participate in a tour of the bus to the West Coast. I made an agreement with Reverend Hutchings to pay the difference of towing the bus between two of the other locations already on their tour, which was scheduled for the winter of 2004-5. Reverend Hutchins told me that someone in the Bay Area Jewish community called him to offer money to not send the bus to Berkeley. The offer was higher than the amount that I had already paid. Reverend Hutchings rejected the offer.

Bombed Bus #19

Preparations for Bus 19 Rally

The Israel Action Committee of the East Bay (IACEB) went into high gear to organize an anti-terrorism rally in the Martin Luther King Jr. Memorial Park in Berkeley. IACEB needed to accomplish the following: get a permit for the rally, rent the park, get a sound permit for amplification, raise money to tow the bus to Berkeley, get a security team to protect the demonstrators, provide a medical team in case of injuries, find and invite speakers, locate a parking place for the bus's overnight stay before the rally, make posters, advertise the rally, find parking for the attendees, and complete a myriad of other tasks, to bring this project to fruition. I had never undertaken such a project before and had no experience with how difficult it was going to be. Every day there was a new administrative requirement from the City and strong opposition from the Jewish community. The City also required my posting a million-dollar bond to cover any damages to the park and its surroundings. It was gratifying that several organizations, such as Democracies Against Terrorism (DAT) and Schindler's Ark co-sponsored the rally.

Opposition From The Organized Jewish Community

From the beginning it became clear that the organized Jewish community would have nothing to do with the Bus 19 project, and that it would create roadblocks to make it fail. For example, the Rabbi of my Synagogue, Beth Israel, refused to say *Kaddish* at the rally for the bus victims. Rabbi Stuart Kelman of Netivoth Shalom, where was also a member, told the congregation: "I personally, will not attend and ask you to stay away as well." Only Rabbi Ferenc Raj, spiritual leader of Temple Beth El, attended the rally, together with Temple Beth El's sister black church. None of the Jewish organizations in the East Bay allowed Bus 19 to park in their parking lots the night before the rally. I was shocked that these organizations were frightened of supporting a "Stop Terrorism Rally." An article in the *Berkeley Voice* by columnist Martin Snapp quoted Ramiz Rafeedie, a spokesman for the Bay Area chapter of the American Arab Anti-Discrimination Committee: "Palestinians can barely get their children to school, much less to the streets of Berkeley to tell their side of the story." Susan Green, president of Jews for a free Palestine, agreed his point of view. "It is mean to demonize Palestinians and deflect the American people away from the fact that millions of tax dollars are spent daily to support the illegal occupation of Palestine."

Preparing For the Rally

Our peace rally was held on Dr. Martin Luther King's birthday, January 16, 2005, and succeeded beautifully in spite of the opposition. Over 500 people attended, and was covered by many TV and radio stations. The City of Berkeley delayed issuing a permit until three days before the event, although I had initially requested the permit four months before. The city demanded that we post "No Parking" signs all around the park for three days before the rally but, because of the MLK holiday, the City's parking office was closed, and I could not get the signs. How I got all one hundred of them is a secret. No—I didn't break into the Parking office! Hugh and I, along with a friend, posted the signs, which took half the night. The permit required the setting up of barricades, but the Police Department did not set them up. Volunteers who were on the street early on Sunday morning helped us carry the heavy metal barricades from the police department to the park and helped erect them in the park to separate the rally from the protesters.

We were ready for our rally but had no place to park or hide Bus 19 during the pre-rally night. Berkeley would not allow us to park the bus on the site, as the permit was for only 3:00 AM to 5:00 PM for that Sunday. Fortunately, a Christian organization led by Dr. Rosemary Schindler, Schindler's Ark, allowed us to park the bus in their lot during the night before the rally. One of our group infiltrated an anti-Zionist organization and dropped a red herring, telling them that the bus was in a different location. The roadblock that the Palestinian protesters organized blocked the wrong freeway. We assembled a group of drivers who would escort the bus across the Oakland-Berkeley line, as Berkeley would not allow the bus to cross the city border without an escort. When we brought the bus to the designated parking spot near the park (it was not allowed into the park), we found that there were cars and trucks parked in our "No Parking" space. The vehicles belonged to a volunteer service that fed breakfasts to homeless people, and they promised to leave before our rally. We apologized to the homeless people for asking them to leave, and they were very forgiving and kind and even helped us erect the barricades before they left.

Rally Protesters

Numerous cars carrying pro-Palestinian demonstrators honked their horns to drown out our speakers and drove by next to the park and the Police station but were not given tickets or arrested. Anti-rally protesters broke through the barricades (they had no permit for use of the park or for sound amplification) but were not arrested or given citations. Instead, one of our own group was arrested for arguing with a protester. Pro-Palestinian protesters using amplified sound equipment were yelling right in front of the police department without any interference from the police.

Speakers and Volunteers at The Rally

We were very delighted to have Berkeley Mayor Shirley Dean give a powerful speech at the rally. Rabbi Cooper of the Simon Wiesenthal Center flew from Los Angeles to recite Kaddish for the people who were murdered on the bus. Journalist David Bedein arrived from Israel to give an emotional speech. The Swaranjali Youth Singers, an Indian group, sang beautiful songs including Amazing Grace. Electrician Robert Fliegler set up the sound system at no cost.

Numerous TV channels and a wonderful radio host, Jeff Katz, of a San Francisco radio station, KPIX, conducted a lively broadcast with call-ins. Videographer Esther Andrews made a documentary from footage filmed by filmmaker, Mary Jean Gunden.

My good friends, Thalia Broudy and her husband, Bob, were available at all times to work on and help produce the rally. Gina Waldman of JIMENA (Jews Indigenous to North African Lands) spoke eloquently. Nonie Darwish, a North African Jew, from her organization "Arabs for Israel," was also a speaker. David Meir-Levi served as the Master of Ceremonies. An amazing speaker, Walid Shoebut, a former Palestinian terrorist, from Bethlehem, who had converted to Christianity, spoke passionately about ending terrorism. Dr. Rosemary Schindler of the Shiloh Church and Schindler's Ark were the key to the success to the rally. Reverend Schindler spoke eloquently, helped hide the bus, made important contacts for our group and gave us invaluable advice and help. A volunteer from the Christian community blew a Shofar to call people to pray. Many of my friends, including Lisa and Bob Cohen of San Francisco Voice For Israel, Dr. Mike Harris, and many others, were vital to the success of the rally. The rally was co-sponsored by DAT (Democracies

Against Terrorism) and Schindler's Ark, among other organizations.

Bus 19 Getaway

A group of our friends used their cars to block the hostile demonstrators from following Bus 19 to its next destination. They unblocked Allston Way soon after the bus was towed away. The Bus went to San Francisco for a second rally, which was organized by the San Francisco Voice for Israel, led by Dr. Michael Harris and Dr. Dan Kleiman. The SF rally was well attended by immigrant Russian Jews.

We were fortunate to have a talented videographer, Mary Jean Gunden, who expertly photographed the three-hour long rally and managed to shoot crowd scenes and record all of the talks. Ms. Gunden had the help of many volunteers who helped introduce the speakers, provide excellent sound amplification and hold back the crowds so that she could photograph everything. Ms. Gunden was unable to find time to edit the video so it was completed in its finished form by videographer Esther Andrews who produced a dramatic and polished record that showed the attempts to shut us down. We had sponsorship from DAT (Democracies Against Terrorism) and Schindler's Ark.

IACEB submitted the documentary film, Bus 19, to the San Francisco Film Festival but it was not accepted. The film festival for 2005 was held in a theater on the same street that the rally had been held and many local people were featured in our film and would have attracted many attendees but the reason given by the then president of the SF film festival was that it was not technically good enough. I feel that it was an excuse to cover their political bias. I hope that the rally had some positive effect in informing local Bay Area residents of the horror of terrorism, but I know that such acts still occur, which makes me very sad. Tragically, terrorism is still a daily occurrence in the world.

The beginning of the video shows pro-Palestinian protesters yelling right in front of the police department that is right across the street from Dr. Martin Luther King Jr. Park. The protestors had no sound permit – only I had a sound permit for the event. The Berkeley police issued no citations. I should have registered a complaint that the protestors had no sound permit but were not cited violations such as honking their car horns, shouting epithets and being disruptive but I was so exhausted the I didn't follow through.

Hugh felt very uncomfortable at Livermore Laboratory that continued to harass him. He disagreed with their nuclear bomb projects and was outspoken in trying to prevent nuclear testing. He was able to obtain a sabbatical leave in 1989 and fill the year with three appointments; the first was at the University of Rochester, in New York; the second was being the director of a three month international workshop in theoretical physics at the University of California in Santa Barbara; and the last third was a teaching appointment at the University of California in Santa Cruz. I did not join him his term at Rochester as I was still employed in my own profession but I visited him in Rochester where we took a marvelous and romantic trip to Niagara Falls and Canada, both very beautiful. A very good friend of mine who is a pilot flew me to Santa Barbara where I spent an exciting week meeting fabulous people at the conference. I enjoyed the last third of the year when Hugh was at Santa Cruz and was able take weekend trips home to Berkeley. Hugh rented a room from Joel and Glenda, very close to the beach, and we were able to watch the sea lions and hike along the shore.

Hugh's Scientific Career

Hugh continued his research in astrophysics and stellar evolution along with his efforts to end atmospheric nuclear testing. He was invited to many conferences that were arranged by the Pugwash group, named after the town in Nova Scotia that received a Nobel Prize for its anti-nuclear proliferation agenda. The Pugwash conference on Science and World Affairs is an international organization that brings together scholars and public figures to work toward reducing the danger of armed conflict and to seek solutions to global security threats. It was founded in 1957 by Joseph Rotblat and Bertrand Russell in Pugwash and supported by Albert Einstein.

Hugh attended many Pugwash conferences that were held in Germany, England, Germany and other countries. I was lucky to be able to accompany him to conferences and meet other scientists who wore working on ending nuclear weapon proliferation. It was very heartwarming to watch these dedicated scientists struggle to put an end to atmospheric nuclear testing and establish protocols for world peace.

City of Berkeley Peace Prize

In September of 1986 Hugh was awarded, to his great embarrassment, The Berkeley City Peace Prize, for his pursuit of peace. It was a lovely award for his being an outspoken critic of the Lawrence Laboratory's weapons development and his decades long and courageous battle to stop activities to stop atmospheric testing. It was a wonderful recognition but the award from Crazy Berkeley was extremely awkward. Our friends all laughed about it and teased Hugh endlessly.

Visit to Eastern Europe and Poland
in 1989

Hugh was invited to a Pugwash meeting in Berlin in 1989 and we were able to explore Berlin during the time that the wall came down and travel between East and West became possible. The wall had been erected on August 13, 1961 and we had heard the news while I was in the hospital giving birth to Joel. Ironically, the wall fell on November 9th, coincidentally the anniversary of *Kristallnacht*, when the head of the East German Communist Party announced that citizens of the GDR could cross the border whenever they pleased.

We rented a car in Berlin and, with our close friend and Hugh's colleague, Dr. Martin Kretschmar, we traveled through East Germany to Poland. There was no barrier or checkpoints between the countries. We saw many old Trabant cars traveling west and many returning east with roof carriers piled high with western commodities.

Our destination was Lug, south of Warsaw, where there was an international physics conference to which Hugh had been invited. The conference was held in a private mansion belonging to a former nobleman that had been re-purposed into a convention headquarters. I was able to spend time with the housekeeper and cook while we traveled from village to village in order to buy groceries. I was shocked to find that the stores were empty of goods, or were even closed. It was terribly difficult to buy anything in stores at that time. Eventually the cook was able to buy groceries directly from farmers so the conference meals were tasty and nutritious. Farmers transported their goods on horse pulled carts. Pigs and chickens ran freely in the streets. It felt as though I had stepped into the previous century.

Hugh and I drove to Warsaw and searched for the former Warsaw Ghetto in the old Jewish quarter, but were unable to locate it. The Ghetto uprising, in July 1943 was a revolution in European Jewish history where the starving and sick inhabitants rose up to die fighting and inflict injuries on the enemy. Over 300,000 Jews had been deported to Treblinka from the Ghetto in the summer of 1942. There were some signs in the large square in the city that seemed to locate the Ghetto, but we never found the exact location. There was an art exhibit in one corner of the central square where I found a picture of four old men with black hats and hooked noses counting coins. It was a typical stereotype of Jewish misers.

After the physics conference we drove to Krakow and we saw several buildings that had been Synagogues converted into factories. We stopped at one of the buildings with Hebrew script and a Jewish Star on the façade, and found that it was now a factory manufacturing latex gloves. We stayed at a grungy old hotel in Krakow that had a poster on the wall listing tourist sites. One of the sites listed was Auschwitz. A tourist sight? I was very offended. Auschwitz is much more than a tourist site.

Auschwitz and Birkenau

We visited Auschwitz to say Kaddish for the many people who were murdered there, including my relatives. A man with a taxi solicited us to take a tour but I declined as I felt that no one should make money of this tragedy.

The day that we visited Auschwitz was stormy and rainy

with thunderclouds threatening a lightning storm. The parking lot was empty except for several Italian school busses carrying teenagers on a trip to understand the Holocaust. The students erected a statue in front of a memorial. They held a service, sang songs and dedicated the sculpture. Just as they said a blessing for the victims there was a loud thunderclap with lightening, and the sky opened up and poured rain. The students stood still in the rain and endured the discomfort. It was a very moving sight.

The vastness of the camp was astonishing. Of the wooden barracks that had housed the prisoners, only the brick chimneys remained. Crows perched on top of the chimneys, an ominous vision. The crematoria had been blasted to bits by the Russians. We said Kaddish for the murdered Jews, Roma, Gays and other Nazi victims. Hugh and I were sickened by the tragedy and horror the place represented. Starvation, illness and beatings with no escape except for the gas chambers or shootings were not news to us but being in the actual location was a nightmare. There are no words to adequately describe what we felt. I had an experience of a mixture of terrible sadness for the victims and guilt that I had survived. For what reason was I still alive? What must I do to justify my existence?

Czechoslovakia and Return to Germany

We crossed from Poland to Czechoslovakia that no longer had border patrols and visited the beautiful Czech countryside. The towns were lined with cobblestone streets and offered passable restaurants with great paprikash and delicious pastries. Streetcars rattled noisily on their tracks all night but we soon got used to, and even enjoyed, the racket. When we arrived in Prague and were amazed to see the beautiful architecture still intact in the old parts of the city. The town squares were full of venders, markets, strollers and even demonstrator. We stayed at guesthouses outside Prague that were cheap and had great beer.

Many of the locals spoke German because there was a large German population living there before the Nazis invaded.

We continued our drive back to Germany where we visited the Brandts, the family who hosted Hugh in his student days. Mrs. Brandt had passed away and Dr. Brandt had remarried, which alienated his sons. His health was in decline and he barely recognized us. It was a sad reunion. We flew home after that.

Our Careers

Hugh continued a productive career in physics at the Livermore lab continuing his research on astrophysics and editing physics papers sent for review from journals. I continued to work for the biotech company, Xoma, until I was fired by a newly hired supervisor who didn't know any science and with whom I clashed. After losing my job, I filled my time with auditing courses, writing my pro-Israel newsletter three times per week, gardening, folk dancing, volunteering, catching up on reading and taking my Bernese Mountain Dog, Serena, for long hikes.

Taking Granddaughter, Raizel, to Israel

Our grandchildren were now in their teens and I decided to take our eldest granddaughter, Raizel, to Israel in order to attend an *Ulpan*, a total immersion Hebrew language school that was located in Netanya. Raizel was fifteen years old and very mature and I thought that it would be fun to spend time on the Ulpan with her and then tour Israel together.

Raizel was delighted to come with me and we flew to Israel in September of 2009 to attend Ulpan Akiva located near the beach resort of Netanya. The housing at the Kibbutz that hosted the Ulpan was full so we stayed at the Palace hotel near the beach in Netanya and were picked daily up by a shuttle taxi. The sessions went from 8 AM to 1 PM with lots of homework for the afternoon. There were frequent programs about Israel in the evening. Raizel was a whiz at acquiring Hebrew and finished her homework promptly and was off to the beach or town and made friends easily. We both enjoyed the beach, the city of Netanya, and the evening programs.

Our class was a mixture people with several Hebrew levels. Some students were immigrants who wanted to improve their fluency, and others were new immigrants who were just beginners. A diplomat from the Norwegian consulate, who already spoke fluent Hebrew, was in an advanced class. There was a friendly and kind Palestinian doctor who worked in an Israeli hospital in our section. He had brought along his wife and baby daughter. A large group of French families participated (not Jewish, I believe) who wanted to settle in Israel participated in the advanced group. They were very studious and hoped to settle in Israel together and start a community business.

A Tragic End to Laila's Life

Late one afternoon during the fifth week of our study, I received a phone call from Hugh giving me the terrible news that Laila had killed herself. I could not absorb what Hugh said and gave the phone to Raizel and she confirmed the dreadful news. We checked out of the hotel immediately and called for a taxi to go to the airport and made arrangements to return home. The personnel at the Ben Gurion airport in Tel Aviv were helpful and sped us through formalities and arranged for a flight to San Francisco. We were hustled through security without security checks and embarked on a plane that had been held on the tarmac for us. The airport employees were sympathetic, efficient and kind.

It was a great comfort to have Raizel with me and she instinctively knew when to let me talk and when I needed to be silent. The flight seemed eternally long and exhausting and I alternated between grief and numbness. I was relieved that we were met by Hugh and our sons when we arrived in the San Francisco airport. I was emotionally drained and in shock and hardly able to function. Hugh explained what had happened, but I could not assimilate the details, nor did I even want to hear them.

The Rabbi of our congregation, Yonatan Cohen, came to our home and helped organize the funeral. He was very sensitive and caring and shouldered the burden of making arrangements and initiating calls to key people to be present at the funeral. The Hebrew teacher who taught Laila her Bat Mitzvah portion offered to conduct the services. Pete, Laila's partner of 20 years, came and gave us emotional support even though he was in need himself.

We believe that it was a sudden impulse, a copycat self-destruction at a train/road intersection in Mountain View where several other suicides had taken place in the previous weeks. All of the victims had thrown themselves under trains. Laila had been clean of drugs, working at a job and had a date with Hugh for lunch the following day. I think that the struggle to stay clean of drugs was unbearably hard and led to her despair.

A large group of people who were friends of Laila's came to the funeral and told us how they loved and admired her and what an inspiration she had been as a dancer and how they wished that she were still among us. Pete was a wonderful friend but she just couldn't cope with a drug-free life. We were devastated to lose our beautiful, talented but troubled daughter, and I miss her every day.

Our Life After The Loss of Laila

At first we spent time answering condolence letters and calls and spending time at our congregation taking courses in Jewish studies. After the 30 days of mourning (the *Shloshim* period) we tried to manage to continue our lives, spend time with Pete, and enjoy our grandchildren. This was very healing and we managed to get through this terrible period. I kept wondering if Laila had suffered but Hugh tried to put it out of his mind. We continued to go to our music and drama subscriptions and visit with good friends and, after a while, we were able to go to Yosemite, our favorite park, and hike and relax. After a while, we were able to enjoy our lives again, especially when we spent time with the grandchildren.

Hugh was still greatly involved in his astrophysics research and continued to serve as an editor and reviewer for many physics journals. He drove to the Livermore Laboratory daily and continued on in his thriving professional career. I devoted myself to pro-Israel activities and e-published my Israel-activist Newsletter three times per week to a huge subscription list. I attended every pro-Israel event or lecture that was available and went to political meetings and events. Both Hugh and I attended

276

grief groups and found some helpful but others useless. Help came from the understanding that many parents experienced the loss of children by suicide and were all loving, conscientious and caring parents. There were no traits in common among the parents that led to the tragic outcome of their children's lives. They were all emotionally devastated and tried endlessly to understand what had gone wrong. I understood that neither Hugh nor I were able to counter Laila's unhappiness. The times, drug culture, peer pressure and, perhaps, brain biochemistry contributed to the tragedy.

Hugh's Last Few Years

Hugh had had asthma all of his life and also suffered from sleep apnea. He was susceptible to colds and he suffered from bouts of pneumonia. In his late seventies he was subject to breathless periods and felt quite weak. He was diagnosed with cardiac irregularities and atrial fibrillation that resulted in in a general physical weakness and eventually an inability to walk well. He received a pacemaker, cardiac ablation, many medications and treatments that ultimately sapped his physical strength. He was mentally clear and productive but he suffered from physical weakness. This was very strange to him as he had been a strong man with huge energy. He was very disappointed that he didn't even have the strength to walk.

At age 83, he suffered from build-up of fluid in his chest and was subjected to fluid extractions on a weekly basis at Alta Bates Hospital. It seemed to be a routine procedure to Hugh, but it took its toll. One night I woke at 2 AM and found him unresponsive. The medical responders who arrived shortly after my discovery said that it was too late to revive him and I had to accept that he was dead. My two sons quickly came to our house and spent the rest of the night with me. I was very grateful and I depended on their strength and support. I also leaned heavily on my congregation, Beth Israel, and Rabbi Yonatan Cohen. He was marvelous and arranged the memorial service and the burial although he could not personally attend because he was a Cohen, a priestly class who are not allowed to enter graveyards. Many friends, relatives and colleagues came to pay their respects. It was a comforting moment. Ralph and Joel delivered beautiful eulogies that showed their great love and respect for their father.

One Of Hugh's Last Emails To A Friend

"The Lab really treats me well——office, ample computer time, facilities,——but I really have no one to talk to about physics, and my time is filled up with too many medical appointments to really get anything done. So I am going to start moving books and some folders from LLNL to home in Berkeley, and phase out of the Lab by this coming summer. Whatever I do from now on is for personal interest and for my own pleasure. There is no point in continuing the 43-mile commute, and Sanne needs me more at home.

Best wishes,

Hugh

My Adjustment After Hugh's Death

It was a dreadful time. Hugh and I had been married for 58 years and I could not imagine a life without Hugh. I felt abandoned, distraught, frightened and alone. I had my sweet and gentle Bernese Mountain Dog , Serena, and we went on long hikes. She was a wonderful companion, very sensitive to my moods, and very loving. She would put her head on my lap and look at me sorrowfully. She was a great comfort.

I was afraid of preparing tax returns, executing contracts, banking, house upkeep and car maintenance and I felt lost and sure that I could not manage. Eventually I just carried on with the help and advice from my sons who were very generous with their help and expertise. I have made some mistakes but I think that things are in order. I spent many sleepless nights worrying unnecessarily. There isn't a minute that I don't miss Hugh.

It took me a long time to dispose of Hugh's clothes and I haven't yet begun to organize Hugh's scientific and political papers. I hope that my sons will help as they majored in physics and can understand how to organize Hugh's immense scientific output. I miss Hugh's advice, physical closeness, good humor and, most of all, his company. I have many friends and am not lonely but I still long for Hugh. I don't like sleeping alone and my kitten, BonBon, sleeps on the bed, bites my toes and purrs. That helps.

The Present

I am now 83 years old, approximately the same age as the residents in the *Altersheim*. I am still living independently and am able to drive and can enjoy a full and active life. When I look back, I feel incredibly lucky. Many people risked their lives by helping me escape from Germany. Many more were welcoming and supportive in the various countries I lived in after my escape. I am incredulous at the generosity and kindness of many friends, teachers and employers who made my life a rewarding and prosperous experience. I am most grateful to Hugh, my husband of 58 years, who was always kind, supportive and loving and who made me feel treasured. I can't believe in my good fortune in having met Hugh, when I was 18 year of age and that we were able to have careers and raise a wonderful family. I miss him terribly and treasure my memories of our lives together. I think of Hugh every minute and am still inspired by his productive life. I am constantly inspired by the wonderful people who saved my life. There are many good people on this earth.

Sanne

References

Summer of Love

The Summer of Love was a social phenomenon that occurred during the summer of 1967, when as many as 100,000 people, mostly young people sporting hippie fashions of dress and behavior, converged in San Francisco's neighborhood of Haight-Ashbury.

Wikipedia: https://en.wikipedia.org/wiki/Summer_of_Love

The So-Called "Polenaction" - The Expulsion of Polish Jews From the Reich, 1938/1939

https://yvng.yadvashem.org/nameDetails.html?language=en&itemId=1709933&ind=2

http://www.holocaustresearchproject.org/ghettos/piaski.html

https://www.bundesarchiv.de/DE/Navigation/Home/home.html

https://www.bundesarchiv.de/gedenkbuch/zwangsausweisung.html.en?page=1

https://www.google.com/search?
q=Katzenstein&oq=Katzenstein&aqs=chrome..69i57.1183j0j7
&sourceid=chrome&ie=UTF-8

The Blitz, World War II

https://www.britannica.com/event/the-Blitz
"The Blitz, (September 1940–May 1941), nighttime bombing raids against London and other British cities by Nazi Germany during World War II. The raids followed the failure of the German Luftwaffe to defeat Britain's Royal Air Force in the Battle of Britain (July–September 1940). Although the raids caused enormous destruction and heavy civilian casualties— some 43,000 British civilians were killed and another 139,000 were wounded—they had little effect on Britain's ability to continue in the war and failed in its immediate purpose of dominating the skies in preparation for a German invasion of England."

Records of WW2 civilian war dead published online

https://www.telegraph.co.uk/history/world-war-
two/10454718/Records-of-WW2-civilian-war-dead-published-
online.html

History of the Jews in the Netherlands: Breakdown of Deportations from 1940-1945

https://en.wikipedia.org/wiki/History_of_the_Jews_in_the_Ne
therlands#Breakdown_of_Deportations_from_1940-1945[33]

Documentary Video of the Bus 19 Rally

https://youtu.be/U9yrXzXu3SQ

About the Author

Susanne (Sanne) Kalter DeWitt, a Jew, was born in Munich, Germany in 1934, the beginning of the Nazi era. Her parents were Dr. Samuel *Simche* Kalter and Klara (nee Katzenstein.) Sanne describes her deportation to Poland and her arrest on Kristallnacht, followed by incarceration in Dachau concentration camp.

Sanne escaped from Germany at the age of four with the help of a gentile woman and was hidden in Holland. A year later she was sent to England on channel ferry and survived the London Blitz of 1941. She spent most of the rest of WW2 in a South Wales mining village.

Sanne and her parents immigrated to the United States in 1945 where her parents struggled to regain their professional lives and become U.S. citizens. She received her education at the City College of New York, Cornell University and completed her graduate work at U.C. Berkeley where she studied microbiology and genetics.

One of Sanne's passions in life is to dispel the toxic concept of "Race" for which there is no biological basis, with its resulting prejudice and hatred. Her response to people who express racist ideas is: "We Are All Members of the Human Race." Her other passion is support for Israel Advocacy. She founded the organization "The Israel Action Committee of the East Bay" and e-publishes a newsletter about Israel and anti-Semitism three times per week that is sent to a large list of subscribers. She is also very proud her three grandchildren who are in college. One granddaughter is currently applying to medical school.

Sanne's late husband, Dr. Hugh E. DeWitt, was an astrophysicist who fought courageously against the nuclear weapons development during his employment at the Lawrence Livermore National Laboratory (LLNL).

Sanne and Hugh raised three children in Berkeley while she was in graduate school and, later, working in the biotechnology industry developing treatments for cancer and infectious diseases.

Sanne's hobbies include gardening, Israeli folk dancing, traveling, protesting anti-Semitism and being on the boards of several pro-Israel organizations. She is a member of Berkeley's Congregation Beth Israel, a Modern Orthodox Synagogue.

Made in United States
North Haven, CT
07 May 2024

52229837R00181